Wrinkled
Sheets and
God's Grace

Books by Doreen Priscilla Brown

Poetry Speaks

Move Mountain Move

Touched By A Galilean

Wrinkled Sheets and God's Grace

Wrinkled Sheets and God's Grace

Reconciliation. Restoration.
Reclamation.

DOREEN PRISCILLA BROWN

Wrinkled Sheets and God's Grace
Reconciliation. Restoration. Reclamation.

iUniverse books may be ordered through booksellers or by contacting:

iUniverse
1663 Liberty Drive
Bloomington, IN 47403
www.iuniverse.com
1-800-Authors (1-800-288-4677)

ISBN: 978-1-4917-3685-2 (sc)
ISBN: 978-1-4917-3684-5 (e)

Library of Congress Control Number: 2014913505

Printed in the United States of America.

iUniverse rev. date: 08/04/2014

CONTENTS

ACKNOWLEDGMENTS & DEDICATION

Thank you, Father, for the work you are doing in my life! It is because of you that I live, move, and breathe and I'm kept set apart by the power that flows from you. Thank you for your constant reminder that you will always keep me in perfect peace once I remain passionate about you.

I want to acknowledge a number of individuals who have supported me throughout the experience of writing *Wrinkled Sheets and God's Grace:* my close circle of friends, including my adult children, Donny, Deidre, and Kirkland, who "try" to protect me from overworking … Thank you from the bottom of my heart!

I want to dedicate this book to the countless number of single and married women and men—mostly women—whom I've had the honor of sharing ministry with during my various interviews and presentations on the important subject of purity. I have seen your pain—some of it looks exactly like the pain I felt during my challenges with sheet issues. That we have in common from the outset! I've been there, so when I tell you "I feel you," it's not just another cliché—it's from my heart.

There have been times when, like you, I had risen to the mountaintop, and just when I was set to abandon the memory of my valley experiences weighed down with regrets, I found myself right back to where I thought I had risen from. That's when you have to keep a close eye on despair and the Enemy and remember that you cannot allow yourself to fold because the sprint to the finish line is too important.

I heard your would-a, could-a, should-a. You shared stories about your sheet travails, and I listened to the blame and, in some cases, punishment you inflicted on yourself. But let me remind you once again, ever so gently, as best I know: God forgives! That you can count on! He wants so badly for you to hand your sheet mess over to Him and position yourself to dress your bed in fine, spotless linen—that's what He does for His princes and princesses! And make no mistake: you are the apple of God's eye. So bask in the sunshine of His love, and rest on His promises today! He has you covered!

FOREWORD

By Deidré L. Pratt

Founder & President, My Worth Ministries, Inc.

What do you do with your wrinkled sheets blemished by moral blunders and spiritual goof-ups? How can you move on after experiencing moral turpitudes—failure after failure, one broken dream after another? Is it possible to bounce back and fall into the arms of a loving Savior after making a mess of your life?

In *Wrinkled Sheets and God's Grace* Doreen Priscilla Brown skillfully allows her book to underscore the importance of surrendering to the Holy Spirit in intimate matters of the heart.

Wrinkled Sheets and God's Grace is authentic, fiery, and witty yet elegant. Not one line is a dull moment! "You don't sell your milk," the author quips at one point, "let him buy the whole cow." Wow! Sounds all too familiar in our society today where families and children are too often shredded to pieces all because of premature, unwise choices in sheet matters.

But we're occupants in a sinful world and the author acknowledges this, thus she expresses deference for this fact: we've all sinned and have come short of the glory of God—that's indisputable! So what happens when we've made a mess of our sheets, when we've "wrinkled" them in clear defiance of what God really wants for us? She cites example after example of how God in His mercy provides the three "R"s for His children—Reconciliation, Restoration, and Reclamation. *Wrinkled Sheets and God's Grace* delves far underneath the shame of scandalous relationships and dares the reader to surrender all blemished sheets to God and expect His transformation!

I've read *Wrinkled Sheets and God's Grace,* and I can testify that this book is the perfect resource for hope in a hopeless world. It is an easy-to-follow recipe for readers who seek to follow Christ and desire to have Him direct the choices we make in our sheet matters. So, whether you are tussling with fall-out from a break-up, starting out fresh in discovering intimacy, or needing to regroup and retool to achieve a blissful and lasting relationship, *Wrinkled Sheets and God's Grace* will anchor you in the haven of stability that Christ brings. I pray you will let it!

INTRODUCTION

Lord, help me to keep my own life in order, lest after
I have preached to others, I myself become a castaway.
I do not run like someone running aimlessly; I do not
fight like a boxer beating the air. No, I strike a blow to
my body and make it my slave so after I have preached
to others, I myself will not be disqualified for the prize.
(referencing 1 Corinthians 9:26–27)

You have been given a sacred responsibility to control who or what lurks between your sheets—period! Here is the litmus test to see who or what is licensed to reside there. Before you pull out of your driveway to go to work, you routinely invite Jesus to ride with you. Before you leave home for church, you ask Jesus to accompany you and to guard your pew. Before you take your final examination, you ask Jesus to clear away the cobwebs from your mind and help you recall all you have learned. Before you venture between the sheets, I dare you to ask Jesus to bless the proceedings, or do you have to ban Him from any place near your sheets because of forbidden goings-on?

You can't have your cake and eat it too—Jesus will not defend one compartment of your life while you conveniently cut off the blood flow to another. Jesus is recognized as either Lord of everything or nothing! Therefore, if you find yourself engaged in sheet secrets outside the boundaries meant for the "designated" person, your actions are in violation of God's plan for your life and will drastically affect your spiritual and physical well-being.

Next to choosing Jesus as your personal Savior, whom you choose as your life partner is the most important decision you will ever make, so you must dig beyond the surface to discover the most intimate convictions of the individual to whom you are attracted to determine his or her relationship with God. For the Christian, any serious, enduring connection will share core values, including perceptions of God and eternal life. *Wrinkled Sheets and God's Grace* is not a how-to book on finding love, nor does it pretend to tell you where to find it. Those aren't among the author's skill set! This book makes a simple claim: for your relationship to be all God wants it to be, both parties have to be intentional about putting Jesus Christ first and last in all matters and be willing to function under the authority of His statutes. I make no apology for this assertion!

It took me decades to fully grasp the fact that you can take a horse to water but you can't make it drink; you cannot transform an adult into something by wishful thinking. Adults can make adjustments and grow in certain areas, but fundamentally, people are who they are, and when they show you who they are, you must believe them. Nobody told me any of this stuff in my formative years, hence I made a series of novice mistakes; my book is mission driven to help you. Even at the first hint that you are attracted to the opposite gender and long before you become emotionally vested in another person, do due diligence and begin your investigation to determine if and how the other party fits your requirements for a lifelong relationship.

Performing the role of detective and digging into a prospective partner's history is not a romantic gesture—I get that. But who's talking about romance? At this point, it is much too early to engage in the mushy stuff; the truth is that there are some life-and-death questions you need to answer first—for example, am I looking at a person who is completely sold out to God, and does he (or she) have a track record to prove that?

Pay close attention to his value system. If he says he loves the Lord but his track record suggests otherwise, you need to bid him a speedy good-bye. You need indisputable evidence you're on solid footing before you become emotionally invested in a potential partner. Track record!

So much rides on due diligence because a spiritual mismatch is no laughing matter; in fact, it's a major cause of relationship conflicts, so when your partner has a deep-seated relationship with God, no matter what tempests rock your world, your ship will remain steady and intact, and the challenges at the time could even draw you closer to each other because your personal and collective faiths are anchored in Christ.

Partners who have little or no shared spiritual values are inclined in times of crisis to stagger and panic aimlessly hither and yon with no mutual connector, thus making it extremely easy for one or both to leave the relationship.

There's no template that guarantees the success of a relationship, but shared values are fundamental to the cohesiveness of any serious, long-term bond. And in relationships, particularly those in which marriage is the ultimate goal, both parties must be aware of their individual and collective responsibility to God, for God forbid one party should be coaxed out of the relationship by the Enemy!

Someone asked me during my research for this book, "What if the other person decides to become unfaithful to God? To walk away from His statutes?" We encourage. We love. We pray. We allow our lives to be shining examples of what Christ meant in John 13:35 when He wrote, "By this all men will know that you are my disciples, if you love one another." One thing we must not do, however, is allow someone else's apostasy to negatively influence our walk with God.

There's no magic bullet for successful relationships, but if you have paid sufficient attention to those eye-opening, pressure-cooker lessons you have learned, as a blood-bought child of God, you will be brutally authentic with yourself and those around you. You will know that beauty wanes, testosterone slows, health declines, wealth fluctuates, and in-laws bolt when they can't control you. While these harsh realities will naturally affect how happy or unhappy you are, your capacity to serve God uninhibited will remain intact if you and your partner are spiritually melded.

It would be unwise to ignore certain realities, such as cultural and doctrinal differences and core values necessary for establishing mutual ground; however, it is amazing how so many of those misgivings are diminished when common ground between the individuals is synonymous with a committed relationship with God. When couples are involved in a love relationship with God, they will honor their relationship with each other. That's why doing all your unpopular homework up front is critical. There's no point pretending a glass is half full simply to justify satisfying flesh outside God's will. That's not smart. That's denial. That's naïve!

Knock, knock. Who's there? Jesus! Jesus who? *Wrinkled Sheets and God's Grace*! You will chuckle, you will cry, you will have aha moments, and you will say ouch! But when the time comes to decide sheet issues, you'll be intentional about having Jesus guard your sheets. The state of relationships in today's society demands you do.

Why should you care about wrinkled sheets in a world in which just about anything goes and purity seems to be on the brink of extinction? It's because your eternal destiny depends on the collective sheet decisions you make, so you should care!

I have become an unabashed friend of the apostle Paul, who entreats us to learn from others' mistakes and as wise children of God to strive to live in obedience to His statutes: "For everything that was written in the past was written to teach us, so that through the endurance taught in the Scriptures and the encouragement they provide we might have hope" (Romans 15:4).

The clarion call is simple—you don't play roulette with your life, and you definitely don't play games with your eternal destiny. Be keenly aware of sweet nothings slithering from the lips of fine-looking physiques bursting at the seams with lust because their goal is to lure you between the sheets and drop you like a hot potato. A pig is a pig even with cologne and bowtie or with perfume and cultured pearls. Whether you dig it or not, if Jesus is not keeping watch over your sheets, the Enemy will.

I heard you. Not everyone is emotionally equipped to make wise relationship decisions. For a very long time, I wasn't. But things are different in this postmodern generation; there are so many resources available, so much help is right at your fingertips, and so much information once considered taboo to discuss even in private is now debated openly, so regardless of your imperfect nesting or how beaten down you have become because of deep relational wounds and scars, you have a perfect opportunity to turn things around. I pray you will allow *Wrinkled Sheets and God's Grace* to motivate you to make prudent decisions from the outset and avoid lifelong relational blemishes.

Just in case you have already made a mess of things, don't despair—all is not lost. You have the ability with the help of wisdom to step up your game, recalibrate your mind, look away from your quandary, and look toward a forgiving God who will grant to you a complete makeover; you will then be equipped to handle future choices.

I implore you to let God take your ashes and turn them into beauty (Isaiah 61:1–3). Be true to yourself and desperate for God, who will keep you pure and clean until His appointed time for the right coupling. Meanwhile, be diligent about your Father's business and prayerfully restrained about whom you share your sheet secrets with. Be especially intentional about that!

THE LIE

Treacherous and tragic the infernal lie,
When first posed assured, "you'll surely not die";
To earth's first mother, who wondered why,
"Should I not of this tree's fruit try?"
But oh the price that would be paid,
When in the ground was Abel laid.
"From dust to dust" sin's price now bade,
That more would die and live afraid.

Yet many succumb to its beckoning call
As mendacity ruins this terrestrial ball.
Gullible are they who continue to fall
For the lie that summons the coffin's pall.

Yet the Lord assured not all was lost,
For Christ would come and pay the cost.
That we might live, He chose to die
And forever expose that infernal lie!
'Twas Jesus, the Christ, who knew all along
For man, sin's allures were terribly wrong.
And if allowed to forever hold sway,

Sin's nets would be filled on that terrible day.
His gift to believers is certain and real.
Salvation it's called—His loving appeal.
Someday not afar before Him we'll kneel.
The price paid for sin He'll fully reveal.
And as for that treacherous, infamous lie,
Its author we're told will surely die.
In the Lord's kingdom we'll need not ask why.
Only joy shall we know "in the sweet bye-and-bye."

—Hamlet Canosa

Vice President for Education
Columbia Union Conference

Chapter One

SETTING BOUNDARIES

Every word of God is pure: he is a shield unto
them that put their trust in him.
—PROVERBS 30:5

The Enemy is like a bull on steroids trying to rummage through your sheets while telling you how irresistible you are. This is stuff nobody tells you, so you need to pray constantly, asking the Holy Spirit to tame your passions and help you make wise decisions that will affect your life for eternity.

Why would you need a concealed weapon permit if it were prudent to brandish your gun in public? Why would you need the universal standard, God's Word, if you had no objection to running around with Tom, Dick, Harry, and Todd? Your standard is your compass; it allows you a measure of discretion over your body. Grant yourself permission to use your own hand-crafted, personalized selection process to decide whom you will tuck between your sheets.

Why boundaries? Why not let everyone run around like oversexed, out-of-control, lower animals? Why even think about standards, guidelines, and high expectations? Fair questions. Let's look at it this way: this chapter may prove obsolete, even ridiculous to those who want to live in friends-with-benefits relationships with little or no concern about standards or commitment or social, spiritual, or health issues. But most human beings desire committed relationships with some semblance of security and specialness. A woman, as an example, wants to believe that her partner is special to her and that what they have going on between them is exclusive, not distributed around the good-old-girls' network.

In another chapter, we will read about the cow and free milk, and while some of the implications may be immediately apparent, let's think about this: once a cow becomes content with distributing free milk, it finds it difficult or impossible to shut off the supply to the rancher later on. Would you return a soiled mattress thirty days after you bought it and demand a new one? Good luck! There's a prudent reason why your invoice read, "Thirty days—no exceptions!"

No Boundaries, No Recourse

The phone rings at three o'clock in the morning. Its owner rushes to the bathroom for a "break." His or her partner is sufficiently awake to hear the lowered, passionate voice. "It was a wrong number" was the explanation. So that scenario was excused, at least for a bit. Not much said, not much more explanation given, not much explanation offered either.

Night two, again in the wee hours. The same thing happens, but this time the bathroom break is a solid hour. "That was some telemarketing nut." So that was two calls, too many, one would think, but no objection was raised.

This short quotation by an unknown writer is on my wall.

> Attract what you expect,
> Reflect what you desire,
> Become what you respect,
> Mirror what you admire.

It's good advice not only for the couple in the mysterious calls but for anyone who expects to lay a respectable foundation for a meaningful relationship. Set boundaries! What happens when we ignore boundaries and go freestyle? The price of milk drops. Credibility and honor are lost. Respect is diminished.

What's the result? A gradual deterioration in a relationship that you thought was shaping up to be a piece of heaven on earth but is now corrupted with exes, baby mamas, pushing and shoving, and couples slapping each other around.

People are treated based on what they are willing to accept. The same could be said about people in relationships who at the beginning let their guard down and settled for abusive treatment. Whatever you tolerate when a relationship is in its infancy is what you will by default be bound by later on.

The Hollywood Influence on Boundaries

Think about who and what make the magazine covers. Not the couples who attend worship services together each week, nor the soccer mom who puts her career on hold to raise her family. It's always who left whom after a violent spat or who moved out after the other was caught cheating.

After my ninety-four-year-old mother reminded me that disintegration starts on the inside, I realized that society has made a fool of itself that family values once held in high esteem are now considered archaic and in many cases are sneered at. We could lay the absence of clearly defined moral values in our society directly at the feet of an amoral society. Look what happened to the Roman Empire and Sodom and Gomorrah. Did their destruction come from without or within?

I had a conversation with an eight-year-old neighbor who was excited about a tablet Santa had brought him for Christmas. I engaged him in his excited stated as he and his mother were walking to their car. The little boy trusted me enough to let me hold his gadget but nervously held onto my hand while I browsed through it. I enjoyed the little fellow; he seemed well adjusted even if consumed with his toy.

We sometimes say children practice what we say, but not so—it's sometimes more correct to say children are reflections of what they see in their parents. His mother didn't realize she was saying a mouthful when she told me about her son's lack of interest in his baby brother since he'd gotten his new toy. I didn't say it, but I understood the reason for his lack of interest in the newborn: "He plays with the tablet nonstop." Imagine that, an eight-year-old deciding how long he should spend on his new tablet!

> *Train up a child in the way he should go,*
> *and when he is old he will not turn from it.*
> —PROVERBS 22:6

What do unbridled children take into their adult years? They learned that boundaries were not important and that as long as their appetites speak to them, they should answer. They learned that commitment and faithfulness in relationships are worthless. They accept the only standards they know, those fed them by society.

When we understand the huge influence society wields on us Christians, we realize how important it is to instill core values in our children and in ourselves as adults even if those standards are constantly challenged by society. It's a challenge especially because the Enemy has it so orchestrated that the lines between what's off limits and what's permissible is often blurred.

> Christians are increasingly facing social pressure to conform to secular society. They have become so accustomed to hearing of affluent people in immoral situations that it is no longer offensive. The standards of the world invade society across the board, and even in the church eyebrows are no longer raised over

revelations about illicit affairs. Disapproving shrugs and sighs are accompanied by nonchalance and indifference. But God has not moved his goalpost, and His position on moral purity will endure as one of the pillars of His laws. The world may have eroded biblical standards but the inexorable command is still there. "Thou shalt not commit adultery." To Him we must give account.[1]

When we think about the weight and power society wields and how the ways of God have taken a backseat in favor of the more popular ways and mores of the Enemy, it is easy to understand how even committed Christians can find it challenging to stay the course toward moral uprightness. But here is a sobering thought: we must lay down new tracks in our thought processes. Though it might look like the fast-moving things of this world have the upper hand, God's Word is good for yesterday, today, and forever—it cannot change!

> *If you fully obey the Lord your God, He will set you high above*
> *all the nations on earth. All these blessings will come upon*
> *you and accompany you if you obey the Lord your God.*
> —Deuteronomy 28:13

In his *Is American Culture in Decline?* David Callahan wrote, "America has become a culture of cheaters." He made the observation in respect to academic, financial, and professional arenas, but does the concern stop there? Doesn't the same mind-set exist as a culture of cheating in terms of sexual infidelity and purity?[2]

Stranger Danger of Boundaries

She dreamed about the goalposts she had erected, but once she woke up, her dreams were merely mirages. Whether by design or by emotional surrender, the posts had been moved and so had her plans. There was

---

1   The Great Controversy … sacred-texts.com

2   *Is American Culture in Decline?* Greenhaven Press 2005, 87.

still some fight left; she was willing to claw her way back into the relationship for the second time, but this time, it was to the muffled sound of tears. What could have gone wrong so early? I set out to look for answers for how a whirlwind relationship could dwindle so quickly and stumbled across some insightful pearls from a website on "What Men Really Think about Sex on the First Date."

> If a guy fulfills his sexual needs too early, it can muffle the call of his own heart. Before he can relate sex to intimacy, a man must first be made to feel; without feelings, sex is only about conquest and relief. One way to try to get him in touch with his feelings is not to put out on the first night.[3]

This quote doesn't represent every man, but it brings to mind what happens when riders put carts in front of horses. In the case of a literal horse, you could probably lasso him and get him to turn around and begin the journey all over again, but, says family therapist Dr. Linda Mintle,

> In the case of putting out physical passion after the fire is already in full flame, there is little that could be done. You are dating an incredibly good-looking guy. You both feel the attraction building up. What do you do? Now is not the time to decide! It's too difficult to think when passion overtakes you. You must decide before you go on the date what your limits will be.[4]

When you have high standards and know Jesus must be the guardian of your sheets, you trade in the flesh to eventually possess the best God has waiting for you. Paul wrote, "Those who live according to the flesh have their minds set on what the flesh desires; but those who live

---

3   bettyconfidential.com/ar/ld/a/What-Do-Men-Really-Think-About-Sex-on-the-First-Date.html#ouZTuvtikhEUzrbR.99

4   www.drlindahelps.comDating Advice: 10 Dating Tips for Christian Singles.

in accordance with the Spirit have their minds set on what the Spirit desires" (Romans 8:5).

When I advance from the horse-and-cart metaphor to Paul's flesh-and-spirit descriptions, I discover the idea is the same: to arrive at our God-ordained destination, we must buy into His formula. Any departure, though seemingly inconsequential, could significantly distort the path sufficiently to cause us to fall into enemy territory. Dr. Mintle's ten dating tips for the single offers what is inarguably a Bible guide to staying in the boundaries of sexual purity.

> Do not be unequally yoked. Put on the armor of God daily. Put obedience over passion. Physical expression must be appropriate. Limits must be set mutually. Examine your personal motives. Is there too much physical and too little other? Less is better. Be guided by love versus lust. Allow the Holy Spirit to direct and lead you.[5]

What Happens When Boundaries Are Snubbed?

We have all hopefully moved beyond the third-grade antics of a girl passing a note to a boy (or a boy to a girl) that reads, "I like you. You like me?" We no longer trip others in class as a crude way of showing we like them. These activities pose challenges for teachers who must addresses them in the context of kids minding their personal space, but the boundaries in the context of life and death, blessings and the absence of blessings, are much more serious. There's nothing cute about hangovers caused by a series of relationships that have soured so much that the thought of another relationship conjures hysteria.

I remain in the moment because it would be deceptive to suggest that joy is always present in waiting. It's not! We all know the challenges of setting and being faithful to boundaries, but what better way is there to

---

5   Ibid.

weed out the bad apples than by doing so? So many of my high school students tell me that if they played hard to get, their love interest would quickly move on to someone else. Hindsight is twenty-twenty, but one of the greatest myths is that if you refuse to turn over the keys quickly, your love interest will move on to the next customer.

What's even sadder is that this misconception applies to older people as well. You see it all the time—Suzie gets pregnant on purpose so Kevin will hang around. No amount of logic can justify snubbing boundaries. Any justification comes with hidden motives and will soon prove to be of ill effect. The person who moves on because he couldn't get to open the cookie jar at will would have moved on just as easily even after getting the cookie. This myth is perpetrated by the Enemy.

Is there a template for setting boundaries? Does one size fit all? Perhaps not, but boundaries must be set if only to maintain civilization. Relationship experts agree that the exact details of a couple's boundaries may differ but will have one thing in common. "Set healthy boundaries and stay true to them. Make sure you are both living from your core values and not making decisions based on feelings and emotions."[6]

Who Said Setting Boundaries Was Easy?

When we think about the weight and power society wields and how the ways of God have taken a backseat to the more popular ways and mores of the Enemy, it is easy to understand how even committed Christians can find it challenging to stay the course toward moral uprightness. But we must lay down some new tracks in our thought processes. Though it might look like the fast-moving things of this world are having the upper hand now, God's word that insists on obedience is good for yesterday, today, and forever—it cannot change!

---

6   Doc & Aryanna, of The Elffington Post About Us HYPERLINK moralrevolution. com/dating-and-sex/ask-the-team/2011/03/boundaries-ask-the-team

If you fully obey the Lord your God, He will set you high above all the nations on earth. All these blessings will come upon you and accompany you if you obey the Lord your God. (Deuteronomy 28:13)

"Trying to reform our lust is like trying to make a dog into a person," wrote Eugene H. Peterson, who had taught his dog, Pumpkin, all sorts of sophisticated tricks. Despite his efforts, he was unable to keep Pumpkin from acting like a dog.

> She always did doggy things ... she ate things people tried not to step on. She sniffed other dogs in places only dogs sniff. She went to the bathroom in public ... no matter how well I trained Pumpkin, she was still a dog.[7]

God's provision for your protection is His armor. He knew from the beginning that man would have to face the fiery darts of the Devil, so He left us His precious promises to help us fight against the temptations He knew would present themselves. If you have to linger in the moment for concrete assurance that this armor is enough, let Paul's encouragement to the church at Ephesus suffice.

> Finally, be strong in the Lord and in his mighty power. Put on the full armor of God, so that you can take your stand against the devil's schemes. For our struggle is not against flesh and blood, but against the rulers, against the authorities, against the powers of this dark world and against the spiritual forces of evil in the heavenly realms. (Ephesians 6:10–18)

---

7   Eugene H. Peterson, The Message (Colorado Springs) Nav Press, 1993, 1994, 1995, 375 [up].

Chapter Two

Self-Denial: A Panacea for Purity

I will not let anyone walk through my mind with their dirty feet.
—Mahatma Gandhi

*When you decide firmly to lead a clean life, Chastity
will not be a burden on you; it will triumph.*
—St. Josemaría Escrivá

Everything worthwhile, including the desire to remain sexually pure, has its challenges. But staying power is not for cowards; you have to be intentional about your goal as you follow the Master's directives.

Far too many singles and married women are coming from a place of whatever it is society has indoctrinated them with. Fully aware of this, secular society has sold them a bill of goods by coloring their perceptions about what is pure and how their interpretation of purity should fit into their milieu.

For so many of us, societal influence has been so strong that it has colored our worldview, particularly where we stand in terms of our walk with God. Let all women be aware—despite how pressured they feel to go along with the dominant theme of "If you like it, let it kill you," they need to know that no amount of debate over the power of sexual stronghold will ever produce practical solutions for purity. Neither can willpower alone! They have to pull their heads out of the sand—man's cold, tough heart and his refusal to wholly yield his desires to God is the problem.

Now that we understand what's causing decent people to attach so easily to a menacing, hard-hearted, heathen society, how can this cycle of defiance be broken? James warned the Christian Jews struggling with sinful inclinations about the consequences of engaging in worldly, sinful practices.

> Each one is tempted when, by his own evil desire, he is dragged away and enticed. Then, after desire has conceived, it gives birth to sin; and sin, when it is full-grown, gives birth to death. (James 1:14)

Sex is not an evil word because sex is not sinful! Sex is a beautiful thing created by God for the joy and pleasure of man within the bounds of marriage and with the explicit condition that sexual purity within the confines of that union between husband and wife must be maintained (Ephesians 5:31). "Each man should have sexual relations with his own wife and each woman with her own husband" (1 Corinthians 7:2).

But the problem of sexual impurity, like so many other biblical diktats, has left behind a trail of smoke much like the lava that spews from a volcano. And who are the victims? Primarily young women who must struggle to reconfigure their shattered lives, having surrendered their innocence to fit in with society's mantra of "Everyone's doing it."

God's directives are never archaic or trite, so there are serious consequences (though not always immediately evident) to setting aside purity in favor of passion. Recognizing the hurt and anguish that will befall all who fail to stay within the confines of God's guidelines, Paul wrote,

> You should be sanctified that you should avoid sexual immorality; that each of you should learn to control his own body in a way that is holy and honorable, not in passionate lust like the heathen, who do not know God ... For God did not call us to be impure, but to live a holy life. (1 Thessalonians 4:3–5)

The apostle's sacred injunction requires two characteristics: self-control and self-denial; each is crucial to maintaining sexual purity.

In his book *Possessed by God*, David Peterson observed the following about this twin attributes necessary to win the battle of sexual clarity.

> Gaining control over one's body and refusing to use it for self-indulgence expresses a true knowledge of God and his will for human life ... God's initial calling of us "in holiness" is to be the ground and motivation for holy living. God did not call us "for impurity" but, by setting us apart for himself, he indicated his desire for us to live differently, as those who belong to him.[8]

A while back, before I became a vegan, I visited a slaughterhouse much like the ones in the Deep South back in the day. I was looking for a fresh rack of lamb. The experience was one I will never forget, especially because the little bearded fellow waiting on me was wearing an unusual headdress draped down his face and protecting his beard. He knew his craft—slicing and dicing with different knives until he produced what I had ordered. Too many (albeit sophisticated) women present their bodies just like that portion of lamb hanging from a rope in the meat shop. Though the imagery is not tame, it's precisely what's out there in a society that has lost taboos about what's right and wrong, what's pure and defective. Don't you think it's time for the other side of society to take a stand? If it doesn't, all women need to keep this near to their

---

8   David Peterson, *Possessed by God; A New Testament theology of sanctification and holiness*, Intervarsity Press, 1995, 82–84.

hearts: their precious jewel is no rack of lamb, and the butcher's cleaver is not their weapon of choice—self-control is!

Genesis underscores the idea that man was made at a level higher than animals no doubt with the expectation that unlike animals, man would exercise self-control and conduct himself uprightly as God's sons and daughters.

> Let us make man in our image, in our likeness, and let them rule over the fish of the sea and the birds of the air, over the livestock, over all the earth, and over all the creatures that move along the ground. So God created man in his own image, in the image of God he created him; male and female he created them. (Genesis 1:26–27)

The image of God! Awesome man blessed with free will and the ability to assume a mind like Christ's and able to overcome the tempter's snares.

What would happen if every time you were hungry, you reached for a chocolate bar or a bag of freshly microwaved popcorn? The answer is obvious and shocking. In 1 Thessalonians 4:3–5, we are reminded of the importance of self-control if we are to come under the authority of God and receive His favor. It is difficult if not impossible to chase after misdirected sexual itches and serve God at the same time. It would be like trying to fly a kite with a brick tied to it. What message are we sending when we fail to curtail our fleshly desires? Are we making the fatal statements that the Holy Spirit is absent from our lives and that we have surrendered our will to the Enemy? We learn from our experiences or those of others that once the Enemy has "plugged" in our carnal urges like lights on a Christmas tree, it's nigh impossible to reel them in.

This is not a scare tactic; Genesis 1 corroborates it. Just as Satan convinced Eve of the lie that God was "depriving" her of the forbidden fruit that would give her superior intellect, he's managed to play the same prank on God's people in the matter of sex. "God doesn't want you to have fun," the Enemy suggests. Actually, we can rest assured God will never deprive His children of something He has blessed and sanctioned, and there is no reason for us to be cautious about enjoying what God has created as long as our behavior is in compliance with His guidelines. The table is set. Grab your knife and fork. *Bon appetit!*

Benefits of Waiting

Those who choose a pure lifestyle and remain in God's will until His appointed time will enjoy rich, powerful testimonies of the blessings of God in their lives. The myth that virtue can be trampled on one day and recovered the next without messy footprints all over it is a notion hatched by the Enemy; it was maliciously designed to sabotage God's best for His children. The Enemy has an impressive record of time spent in God's presence, so he is keenly aware of the potency of God's love and plans for His children and will subtly woo them away from that arrangement if allowed to.

How can we be certain God's rules and discipline reflect His love for us and His thrill when we obey Him? He says so! Following His counsel will enrich our lives during our time on earth, and a healthy sexual relationship in marriage is a vital part of that enrichment.

We understand there is nothing sinful about sex as long as it's in a marriage relationship. When sex is removed from the context of marriage, it becomes a pretext to the real thing, so removing it from that context (to be used for man's perverted use) is a slap in God's face and a gross injustice to its original purpose. We need only look at the climate in the garden of Eden before Eve took Satan's bait to make an intelligent prediction about where modern society is headed. Whenever society made a mockery of biblical principles, the results were devastating. "Do not be deceived: God cannot be mocked. A man reaps what he sows" (Galatians 6:7).

What's wrong with living it up while you're young and settling down later? That's actually not a trick question; it's a reasonable one. But what should the response be without whacking someone over the head with a Bible?

I once used a purity analogy at a seminar that required a new, self-adhesive interoffice envelope I proposed to send to multiple employees in an office. Basil opens the sealed envelope, retrieves his information, reseals the envelope, and sends it to Wayne. He uses the envelope, reseals it, and sends it to Andrew, and so on to some other recipients.

At that point, an inspection shows that the envelope has some outer wear and tear, but something more poignant stands out—the envelope has lost its adhesive and therefore its value, its wealth.

Similarly, whenever you engage in a sexually intimate relationship, you use up emotional wealth. As you repeat the cycle outside marriage, more and more partners become the recipient of your investment. But watch what happens when you decide to settle down in a permanent relationship. You have little (if any) of your emotional value with which to bond in what was expected to be the relationship of your life.

The part about the adhesive went over well, I hope. Do you realize how difficult it was in the beginning to open the envelope but how easy it became later? What happened to the adhesive? What if I told you it was gone forever? So much for treating sex like reusable adhesive.

The idea of reserving oneself for marriage is a wise one that was echoed throughout the New Testament. Mark 10:7 and Matthew 19:5 agree that in marriage, two become one, joined to each other, committed to each other, and exclusive to each other. That's a benefit worth waiting for! No debriefings about how much adhesive was lost by other's use. No insecurities about who "sealed" the envelope best and where the envelope will end up.

Standing Firm While Waiting

How do we stand on our own two feet when everything and everybody around us seem to be going off in so many directions, none of which are on God's roadmap? It's a fair question, one that cannot be ignored if our girls are ever to be properly prepped for an honorable future worthy of their desires and God's expectations.

Standing on our own two feet requires stamina and purpose. Our foundation must be sound, and our reason for standing must be sure. Here's where we get our confidence to run the race in the face of opposition: we know there is clarity of purpose and confidence in God because He makes our standing possible; therefore, we will win!

> For I know the plans I have for you, declares the Lord,
> plans to prosper you and not to harm you, plans to give
> you hope and a future. (Jeremiah 29:11)

In her book *Raising a Lady In Waiting*, Jackie Kendall described the unwavering resolve of the biblical Ruth to follow the call of God even in the face of unpopular reaction from those in her circle.

> Ruth had a determined heart. The Lord honored her
> faith in moving away from all that was familiar and
> taking a journey toward the completely unknown. Ruth
> did not allow her friends, her old surroundings, or her
> culture's dead faith to keep her from running hard after
> God. She did not use the excuse of a dark past to keep
> her from a bright future that began with her first critical
> choice: reckless abandon to the Lord.[9]

In my book *Touched by a Galilean*, I wrote about taking a stand for Jesus in the face of insurmountable odds. I looked at the story of how God stuck to Shadrack, Meshach, and Abednego in the fiery furnace after they refused to surrender their faith. The three young men did

---

9   31.

not vacillate for even a split second; they faced the powerful King Nebuchadnezzar with unperturbed courage.

> From the moment we take a stand for God, Satan becomes agitated because he realizes that the stand-alone principle is a life-changing testimony.[10]

Is there a lesson we can learn from King Nebuchadnezzar's unperturbed attitude? How can lessons learned help those who have taken a stand to wait for the right man or woman to partner with?

I congratulated one of my brothers for waiting on God for thirty-five years before marrying his soul mate with whom he's had three lovely daughters. When asked how he was able to wait that long, he matter-of-factly said that during the waiting phase he was not simply searching for a woman to marry but for a mother for his children. Powerful stuff!

Barriers to Waiting: The Heart and Flesh at War

Today's postmodern, sexually charged society poses unique challenges for a single woman who often want nothing more than to feel admired by a special someone of the opposite gender. So she goes on a dinner date, and everything seems to gel—until her date pulls up to her house and asks to be invited in "just for a nightcap."(I ran this line by a friend as I was negotiating this piece in my head; she had some advice for women in the dating scene: until they really get to know their dates, they should drive themselves to dinner.)

She's stuck. She doesn't want to offend this potentially wonderful guy, but she doesn't want to risk getting into sheet stuff with him. Something tells her this budding relationship is beginning to look more like a friends-with-benefits deal.

Any guy who really desires a committed relationship will respect her

---

10   *Touched by a Galilean,* 54.

wishes to honor her sheets; otherwise, she's been warned—she's dealing with a taker and not someone likely to honor commitments later.

I searched for a good definition of the word *commitment* for the context here. The *Urban Dictionary* offered me an aha moment: "Commitment is what transforms the promise into reality. It is the words that speak boldly of your intentions. And the actions which speaks louder than words."[11]

"It took me so long to find a decent date, and the thought of losing him drives me crazy." I overheard that right before my college speech class started. Rarely is anything ever revealed about commitment; just about everything is about who's hot and who's not. Some of the girls are only eighteen, fresh out of high school, poised to launch optimistic futures. How do you get them to follow their Christian standards and postpone sheet stuff? It's a battle—I know that because I deal with younger singles as well as older singles every day. The pressure they face is indescribable. Talk about a battle of the wills!

I spoke at an event honoring high school students ready to go to college when the mother of one reminded me of my writing about the three Hebrew boys in *Touched by a Galilean*; she was elated about how it fitted neatly into my mini-talk that was admittedly inspired by sobering research into the "new" sex culture on college campuses. In essence, how can you hold onto your beliefs in the face of astronomical pressures at college? We all have this perception in our heads that we've seen it all so there's nothing that affects us any longer. I found this not to be the case when at the convocation ceremony that afternoon, the graduating student selected to give the closing thoughts remarked that for her, my speech had been a reality check that would cause her to navigate an alternative route. Isn't that what it's all about, a wake-up call to remind us of the importance of dedicating our bodily temples to the Lord with joyful obedience?

The question-and-answer segment followed along the same lines as the

---

11   www.urbandictionary.com/define.php?term=commitment

talk did. When I figured this out, I blew up my research questions to further arrest the graduates' and their parents' attention:

"College fairs and college documentaries—are they a fraud? Do they ever get into the nitty-gritty of what really happens on their campuses? And what happens in the classroom is far cry from simply Statistics and English. Drugs. Sex. Alcohol. Professors who inject young, impressionable, eager minds with skewed ideologies and cleverly constructed lectures designed to make your young adults question their Christian faith."

The discourse that evening was not just a titillating exercise designed to bait spirited feedback. Accounts of sexual escapades on college campuses are real—you couldn't make them up. Summit Ministries released some troubling information: "Statistics show that between 30 and 51 percent of Christian college students will renounce their belief system during their freshman year."[12]

This kind of revelation is difficult to swallow, and parents may want to take a deep breath before dismissing this kind of admission. That's understandable. What parent wants to believe the worst about his or her angel who will supposedly want to wait for Mr. Right? Some of those angels will, but perhaps most won't. That's why wisdom says to snap out of denial and face the music—raising children in this postmodern society is not for the naïve or the faint of heart; accordingly, young people and their parents need to be armed with critical information and not delude themselves with superficialities such as beautifully landscaped campuses. When alarm bells ring, listen.

Moving Forward as You Wait

If such data doesn't arrest your attention, perhaps a moment of prayerful reflection will: how do you maintain a spiritually pure Christian lifestyle

---

12 Summit Ministries blog, April 7, 2004 The Importance of Worldview Training—Summit Ministries www.summit.org/resources/truth.../the-importance-of-worldview-training

while in college and far away from parental and other moral support systems? It can be done. It has been done. Rather than stress over errant lifestyles on campus, consider the following to assist in making a smooth transition from home to college. Join a Christian fellowship group. Attend a church preferably of your faith. Study your devotionals to stay rooted during the week. Maintain a rich prayer life to help keep you in shape for the fight. As a soldier of the cross, you must stand up for Jesus no matter what influencers may present themselves.

> If we are thrown into the blazing furnace, the God we
> serve is able to deliver us from it, and he will deliver us
> from Your Majesty's hand. (Daniel 3:17)

Breaking news! To imply that it's easy or convenient to resist sexual temptations on college campus or elsewhere (especially after having been engaged in sheet stuff already) would be like suggesting that the pounds that took five years or longer to put on can be dropped in a day. It's a struggle. Humans are sexual beings and creatures of habit, and sexual urges are strong when they're left to fend for themselves. But when the consequences of sexual impurity are weighed against the joys that await the Christian who chooses to honor God, who would dare complain about fighting the good fight of guarding the sheets? Keeping ourselves pure is not just an act—it's the whole play, the foundation of who we are and who we hope to become as children of our heavenly Father.

I once stumbled across a church ministry website that had posted intriguing lessons on the connection between the old ancient poem and our fight to remain pure in an increasingly sexualized culture.

> Humpty Dumpty sat on a wall.
> Humpty Dumpty had a great fall.
> All the king's horses and all the king's men,
> Couldn't put Humpty together again.[13]

---

13 www.christianpost.com/news/what-humpty-dumpty-can-teach-us-about-sexual-purity-79593/#mkOAi8UILZcm0G07.99

The takeaway from the illustration were four sobering points.

1. You are fragile. Like Humpty Dumpty, you have a breakable shell that's easily shattered.

2. Watch where you sit. Humpty had no right or reason to be up on that wall.

3. Once you shatter, it's hard to get put back together again.

4. Unlike Humpty, you have hope for forgiveness and restoration after a great fall.

Just as Humpty Dumpty was, families today are in peril. Some think families are near extinction because society has abandoned the basic biblical principles that God in His wisdom has established for sexual intimacy, marriage, and procreation. Society has replaced that with a selfish agenda, so it's not difficult to understand how foolish man has become in thinking he can elevate his selfish reasoning and desires above God's platform at will.

When God sealed Adam and Eve's relationship in the bond of marriage (Genesis 2:24), the command was clear without room for any modification or debate: a man will leave his family, join his wife, and become one flesh with her. One flesh for the marriage bed period.

If you think purity is a concept that can be ignored early in life but then be mysteriously prized at adolescence, think again. That's far too late. Nowadays, young people are sophisticated beyond imagination so that by even ages ten or eleven they understand quite well the nuances of their bodies, and talk about the birds and the bees is almost comedic to them. Scripture reminds us, "Start children off on the way they should go, and even when they are old they will not turn from it" (Proverbs 22:6).

Try putting emphasis on the start-off, otherwise, when you muster the courage to take your blinders off, you will be in for a rude awakening. If that happens, deal with it. In some elementary schools, kids aren't just kids—at ages eleven or twelve, chances are good they're doing adult stuff. Take a walk down the hallway during a change of classes or take a seat at a middle-school lunch table. Girls are no longer talking about who likes whom; it's more like a bar brawl—phrases such as "You'd better leave my man alone" and "He slept with me first" are spoken unabashedly. Many of these students are little princesses at home but little terrorizers at school.

The *Psychology Today* article "Overexposed and Under-Prepared: The Effects of Early Exposure to Sexual Content" offered an alarming insight into the effects of sexually uncensored content in music, television, and other media on children.

> Research shows that children who have sex by age 13 are more likely to have multiple sexual partners, engage in frequent intercourse, have unprotected sex and use drugs or alcohol before sex.[14]

Is much of the sexual acting out by children in their late teens and beyond the result of unwise sheet decisions at ridiculously young ages? If you agree that because of the intense nature of sexual activity it's far better handled by mature individuals, you'll agree that the impact of premature sexual activities might well result in erratic, promiscuous behavior at best. You will also agree perhaps that children should be engaged by their parents about sheet stuff at a very early age in age-appropriate phases.

I remember that when I was thirteen, my older sister and I were routinely dressed in pleated or gathered skirts and knee-high socks, and our long-flowing hair was pulled back into a ponytail or two. We were children and were expected to act as children. There was so much innocence and purity in our lives and that of our friends. My daughter thus wore knee-high socks and ponytails until she was thirteen or fourteen. If that

---

14 Psychology Today, Published on August 13, 2012 by Carolyn C. Ross, M.D., M.P.H. in Real Healing.)

picture sounds like a throwback, throwbacks aren't necessarily negative. Children are children; in no way are they ready for adult behavior. Enough said!

I am not making an altar call, for only God can accurately evaluate the performance of His children, but perhaps some parents need to reevaluate their shabby child-rearing practices. Maybe they slumped into fetal positions during parent-teacher conferences when a teacher or principal sarcastically asked (after a heated exchange between parent and child), "Who is the parent, and who is the child?" Solomon said, "Whoever spares the rod hates their children, but the one who loves their children is careful to discipline them" (Proverbs 13:24). Catch them early, or they will lose you in the home stretch.

The good news is that as you sprint to the finish line, Christ will not leave you without child-rearing aids and a second wind. That's a promise! But the decisive question is this: do you have the courage to accept the addictive nature of secular society's attitudes toward sex, unplug from the worldly trappings that skew your children's perception of life, and plug into God's Word to find a clear, virtuous path for your young gems?

All counsel must be unequivocal. Loopholes must be closed so there's no room for misleading interpretations. We should be cautious about any idea that keeping yourself pure in a thoughtless world is easy. The huge irony is that as soon as you commit yourself to God's thou shall nots, you must expect ridicule as a by-product of that decision.

In his presentation in one of my public speaking classes, a college freshman compared taking a vow of purity to "gays coming out of the closet." At first, you're eyed with skepticism, and then subtle fascination followed by resentment. He was right. After Tim Tebow, the world-famous football player stepped on the football field with John 3:16 tattooed on his cheeks, the December 20, 2012, *Huffington Post* headline read, "NFL's most famous virgin."[15]

---

15 Sunday, April 14?, 2013 by WTM.org Community.

In spite of the derision they may face, God expects those who claim to love and trust Him to stay on the correct path, take up their crosses, and follow Him.

In Psalm 23:3, David offered an interesting adjective to describe the path God wants us to follow: "He guides me along the 'right' paths for his name's sake."

What does the landscape look like along the pathway to purity? It's too often fraught with discouragement. Your corner at lunchtime is sparse. The notes passed around in class aren't sent *to* you but contain stuff *about* you. You're just not the coolest kid in the class, so you have to suck it up and make it through the day. That's what the right path can look like for the young person who determines to obey Christ and remain pure.

But purity isn't like an exam students cram for. Purity is modeled for children first by parents and then by scripture. It's doable and rewarding when you remember who you are and whose you are. "When you decide firmly to lead a clean life, chastity will not be a burden on you: it will be a crown of triumph."[16]

Let this question be asked prayerfully, and perhaps the answer can be found in the anecdote about the envelope losing its adhesive earlier in this chapter; is the alternative to purity a sensible option? This example I've heard in various versions. My younger son was about four when a new toy truck arrived wrapped in a multicolored fastener band. Of course the truck was an immediate hit, but something else caught my attention. Each time Donny finished playing with the toy, he would wrap the band around it to securely fasten it. Months went by, and the routine continued, but I began to notice that fastening the band was becoming more of a challenge; the Velcro had gotten clogged with debris and was not attaching to itself no matter how he pressed the ends together. This anecdote has been spun for generations in various forms (I heard a version of it from my grandmother decades ago), but in this

---

16   St. Josemaría Escrivá.

case, it appeared yet again to pull together two of the most reflective phrases a young or older woman will ever consider: Hallowed space? Unsanitary and ill-advised? That's where the Savior wants you to fix your thoughts, "for God will judge the adulterer and all the sexually immoral" (Hebrews 13:4).

So when you think about allowing that which is forbidden between the sheets, think about the pollution of hallowed space, unsanitary and ill-advised; your conclusion could change your emotional and spiritual landscape forever.

That Blessed Assurance

Many hearts have been broken and many lives have been shattered because of clogged bands, and countless are the trails of regrets and pain. But failures are God's opportunities; you can be assured there's never a time when God will not be willing to replace your spent adhesive with fresh glue. There is no sin no matter how dark, how horrific, that's beyond the reach of the blood of Jesus. Even in your rebelliousness, when you have thrown away your esteem and self-worth, you are never far removed from God's forgiveness and mercy. "Whoever comes to me I will never drive away" (John 6:37). "I will repay you for the years the locusts have eaten" (Joel 2:25). God is waiting. "If we confess our sins, he is faithful and just and will forgive us our sins and purify us from all unrighteousness" (1 John 1:9).

None of us is ever too far from God's reach. That's answered in the beauty of the cross, the beauty of God's love for us, and His willingness to forgive us when we have willingly or unwillingly allowed the "locust" to consume our most intimate internal organ (our sexual treasure). Unlike us, who are limited in our ability to forgive and grant second chances to others, Jesus removes judgment from the equation and offers an unmerited chance for newness: "For all have sinned and fall short of the glory of God" (Romans 3:23). When we come to Christ, we stand as if we have never sinned: "All things are passed away and all things are become new" (2 Corinthians 5:17).

Chapter Three
THE NEST DOES MATTER

One of the greatest travesties in society is the
defection of fathers from the family.
—DOREEN PRISCILLA BROWN

There are only two lasting bequests we can hope to give
our children. One of these is roots, the other, wings.
—HODDING CARTER

Parents preach, but children practice what they see ... Parents'
attitude has a strong influence on their children. Whether the
opinions expressed of yourself or others are positive or negative,
your child will in all probability follow your example.
—KIRKLAND H. PRATT[17]

You can never really know a person without knowing his or her nest. To truly know the person is to know his or her experiences, for they connect you. Who built the nest? What experiences were hatched from that nest? What kinds of affections if any were exhibited in that nest? Were they done openly or were they masked?

---

17   Kirkland H. Pratt, Counseling Psychologist ... *Workshop Notes*, November 7, 2012.

I've had a lot in my nest to overcome. When I share with you an example of negative nesting that has never left me even after all these decades, I mean to help you with your own honest self-examination.

Dad was a good provider. We lived in the Caribbean, and Dad worked in a rural part of central Florida, so he commuted between Vero Beach and Leesburg and the Bahamas. His visits home, though all too brief, were exciting times—a young child's dream. He brought beautiful dresses and patent leather shoes (often too small because Dad always seemed to underestimate how fast we'd been growing). Nonetheless, we wore them to match our beautiful little barrettes and ribbons. But there was another side to my nesting that still saddens me. The day I asked him, "Dad, do you love me?" he glanced at me as if I had uttered an obscenity. "Do you?" I pressed him. Dad had no uncertainty in his gaze. When he demanded I look him squarely in his piercing, light-brown eyes, I intuitively feared what was coming. "Last time I was home, I said I love you to all the children, and if I change my mind, I'll let you know."

Two images—Dad the provider, and Dad the father who lacked affection and empathy. I would have eagerly traded in the bows and cute dresses and shoes for the warmth of my father's embrace. I really would.

> If you don't give your daughter this love, she'll do whatever it takes to get it from some other man. Tell her you love her. I don't care if you think she already knows. Tell her. Tell her every day.[18]

When Parental Love Eludes

Next to your heavenly Father's love for you, the love of an earthly father is the most powerful. And if our heavenly Father is willing to shower us with so much undeserved love, how much more should our

---

18 "HELD by His Pierced Hands" posted Meg Hunter-Kilmer, June 17, 2012; www.piercedhands.com/5-rules-fathers-daughters

earthly fathers shower their little girls with the love they so much deserve? Fathers should tell their daughters that they love them loud and clear!

> You Don't Need a Guy: She needs to hear starting at a young age (but it's never too late to start telling her). She needs to be told a boy doesn't complete her, God does. Chasing or enticing or wanting a guy doesn't make her attractive and it doesn't make her a woman. The only guy she needs in her life for a long time is her Dad or a father figure until God brings her a husband if that's His plan.[19]

For most of us, the scars caused by a missing father's love take time to fade. But for those who present themselves to God for the infilling of the Holy Spirit, God will deliver and heal them and provide the help they need to forgive their earthly fathers; He will engrave their nesting testimony on the wall of deliverance as a witness to the world, and He will delete the sting of their hurt—the vestiges of a fragile nest—from their lives.

When a Ragged Nest Gets in the Way

Ghosts from every childhood have a habit of rearing their ugly heads every now and then, but don't let them paralyze you with fear. Grieve over them, and then give them a final resting place. If, like many, you have become absorbed with mourning over a less-than-perfect nest, you'll never be able to revel in the incredible person those ghosts have helped you become. If you don't give yourself permission to vacate your past, you'll by covert consent dwell in your past and by extension attract who you are. To move on from your past, you have to take a bold stand and exorcise your ghosts. Important to your success is the recognition that you're never alone in that battle.

---

19 Raising Daughters in a World That Devalues Them: 7 Things We ... wearethatfamily. com/.../raising-daughters-in-a-world-that-devalues-them... March 20, 2013.

> Everyone has a certain sort of dysfunction to contend with, and people are all who they are because of it. Dysfunction doesn't necessarily determine our destiny in life. Each person has to learn to heal from a bad childhood and to take their destiny into their own hands. You can become a cripple if you allow your childhood to eat at you for a lifetime ... You cannot allow your dysfunctional family life to take control of your life.[20]

Some years ago, I was on a flight to New York and was browsing through a magazine. My attention was caught by an article about a daughter who had made it big and was enjoying a beautiful life with everything at her fingertips except for one thing—she was haunted by thoughts of what her father's arms might have felt like. Thoughts about that conversation with my father surfaced. Here I was, heading toward my golden years and still pretending I'd gotten over my childhood scars. Though Dad, whom I loved so much had passed, repressed unhappy memories suddenly surfaced. But my curiosity extended beyond that single reflection; I began to think more concretely about the influence of childhood scars on those who suffered from them.

I thought about all the talk today about classroom bullying and promiscuous behavior. While some of that attention might be well placed, certain factors that cause kids to act out must not be ignored. Is a child not being bullied when his or her emotional cries go unheeded by parents? At school? By society? When a father turns a blind eye to his daughter's need for emotional sustenance, that attitude triggers dysfunction; the daughter becomes conflicted about boundaries and timing when it comes to intimate relationships. Let's not ignore the fact that teens' brains are still under construction, so the material used in the building process could make the difference later between an emotionally healthy young woman and one who struggles with painful relational

---

20   Barbara Kasey Smith. Created on: March 04, 2008. Updated: October 30, 2012.

issues. When what you experience causes you pain that numbs you, you truly experience pain. But whether you're pained by abandonment or you're the victim of lack of affection, God wants you to put the past behind you. The apostle Paul wrote,

> Brothers and sisters, I do not consider myself yet to have taken hold of it. But one thing I do: Forgetting what is behind and straining toward what is ahead, I press on toward the goal to win the prize for which God has called me heavenward in Christ Jesus. (Philippians 3:13–14)

That's what Jesus asks of you; He wants your testimony to be raised on His wall of deliverance as a witness.

But forgetting the past is tough. There's a subtle notion that Christians are not really Christians if their past is sordid or if they struggle with temptations of the flesh. But Paul's admission of wrestling with his sinful nature in Romans 7:18–19 gives us hope.

> For I know that good itself does not dwell in me, that is, in my sinful nature. For I have the desire to do what is good, but I cannot carry it out. For I do not do the good I want to do, but the evil I do not want to do—this I keep on doing.

Reaping the Rewards

Even after we've dealt with the realities of a ragged nest, the consequences of sin remain. Just like the gentleman who lost his legs in a crash but later surrendered his life to God, we too must bear sin's consequences. Although God's love erases our past sin, it will not restore the physical harm inflicted on us by our willful disobedience. "For the wages of sin is death, but the gift of God is eternal life in Christ Jesus our Lord" (Romans 6:23).

Sin is rebellion against God. When we decide to dabble in sin, we get "fleshly" pleasures, and that's how the Enemy gets a foot in the door. Soon, it's all downhill from there. Jesus said, "I am the way and the truth and the life" (John 14:6). When we sin, we become separated from God and are left to our own devices—no compass, no hope.

Think of our relationship with God as a parent-child bond. When children disobey, their relationships with their parents become strained. The parents will still love their children and have their best interests at heart, but those children will experience some fallout. They will experience guilt, shame, and a profound sense of mistrust and unworthiness. Can such relationships be restored? Of course, but not without pain, which is necessary if restoration is to ever take place.

So it is with God and us. When we rebel against God's rule, we dissent against the life-giver and experience a death, a brokenness that results in pain. When we return to God, we're restored to spiritual life, communion with God, a sense of purpose and righteousness, and a sense of freedom. The rejoicing father in the parable of the prodigal son said it best when he ran out to meet his wayward son: "This son of mine was dead and is alive again" (Luke 15:24). Think about the rejoicing father in that parable; doesn't he bring to mind how God, our Father, welcomes us home regardless of the circumstances? Even when our nests provided spiritual clarity for us but we spurned it for greener grass, that doesn't matter to God; what He wants to hear more than anything else is "I will arise!"

Some Consequences of Messed-Up Nesting

Whether we're talking about our birth nests or our adult nests, the principles are the same—though God will forgive the effects of our tattered nests, welcome us home, and help us to begin afresh, the realities of the nests we built will dictate certain consequences, including memories that will never completely disappear, ill health resulting from abuse of our bodies, material losses due to gambling perhaps, and emotional scars that will affect our ability to bond intimately between the sheets. None of these problems will disappear easily. The lesson here is that there's wisdom in obedience—the quicker we make that U-turn and head for home, the lighter our penalty will be for our nesting choices.

How to Build

Building a stable nest takes time and prayer. Sometimes, you may have to wrestle with God on the things you will allow your young people to invite in your nest. Worldly music can be a challenge, as can be the language they track into your home. The company they choose might also challenge wholesomeness of your nest.

Sometimes, you may go to God in a particular matter and because the solution is not forthcoming you become despondent—that can happen! But pray you must, and your prayer must not be in isolation—your young people must hear you pray. What's perhaps the most challenging part of the equation is the word no one wants to talk about—*patience*. Sometimes you have to wait; your breakthrough will come when God has finished working out His plan. David pictured it this way in Psalm 27:14: "Wait on the LORD; be of good courage, and he shall strengthen thine heart: wait, I say, on the LORD."

Abraham and Waiting

Abraham, faithful follower of God, fell into the "help God out" trap when he refused to wait and God used the tragic result of his impatience in Genesis 16 to teach us about the consequences of failing to wait on God.

Something about the human spirit makes it difficult for us to put total trust in God even when He makes it clear He will do what He says He will. God's promise to Abraham could not have been clearer when He promised him a child by the right woman, his wife, Sarah:

"And I will bless her, and indeed I will give you a son by her. Then I will bless her, and she shall be a mother of nations; kings of peoples shall come from her." Then Abraham fell on his face and laughed, and said in his heart, "Will a child be born to a man one hundred years old? And will Sarah, who is ninety years old, bear a child?" And Abraham said to God, "Oh that Ishmael might live before Thee!" But God said, "No, but Sarah your wife shall bear you a son, and you shall call his name Isaac; and I will establish My covenant with him for an everlasting covenant for his descendants after him." (Genesis 17:16–19)

Abraham had waited a long time for the fulfillment of God's promise. But as the years flew by and the people ridiculed the "outrageous" notion about God's promised son, Abraham's faith dimmed. Even when he questioned the prudence of lying with his handmaiden, he found himself acquiescing to his wife.

Abraham and Sarah took matters into their own hands; they had gone down the forbidden path; they aborted God's promise. By this act of utter disobedience, Abraham's marriage was messed up, and look at the unintended consequences: Ishmael produced Israel's enemy even to this day.

Application and Assurance

God's promise to Abraham is His promise to us: there are blessings in obedience. But even after Abraham had disobeyed and disappointed God, He did not write Abraham off. Rather, He pursued him, and eventually, God revealed His plan to him. Abraham witnessed the end result of the promise in Ishmael even as He reaffirmed His promise.

Abraham said to God, "Oh that Ishmael might live before Thee!" But God said, "No, but Sarah your wife shall bear

you a son, and you shall call his name Isaac; and I will
establish my covenant with him." (Genesis 17:19)

It seems that God was developing Abraham's faith rather than merely
punishing him, for when the pivotal test came to offer up Isaac as a
sacrifice, Abraham aced it! In response, God blessed Abraham.

> I will greatly multiply your seed as the stars of the
> heavens, and as the sand which is on the seashore; and
> your seed shall possess the gate of their enemies ... And
> in your seed all the nations of the earth shall be blessed
> because you have obeyed my voice. (Genesis 22:15–18)

What's the message here? Though God's love for His children is
unconditional and He will never abandon them, there is a high price
to pay for disobedience. God will forgive, but the consequences for
sins must be felt. God tells us to honor our bodies—flee fornication,
let every man have his own wife, marriage is honorable, the bed must
be undefiled—so when we ignore God's instructions and violate the
sheets, our behavior starts the dominoes falling, which we will have to
deal with for the rest of our lives.

Surrendering Your Nest

No nest is so ragged, tattered, or dysfunctional that God cannot rebuild
it. He has done it before and can do so again. You have to give yourself
permission to be released from your dysfunctional nest and find liberty
from your destructive feelings. It's like a caterpillar morphing into a
butterfly. The metamorphosis is not instant—a tiny egg turns into a
larva, which morphs into the pupa, a real butterfly waiting to spread its
wings and fly. The final stage is an adult butterfly, ready to take on a life
of its own. Each step in this metamorphosis is gradual.

Learn a lesson from the caterpillar and the butterfly. As you're
surrendering your nest, you'll become discouraged when changes aren't
instant, but if you're committed, you'll get back in full fellowship with

God; you are His child with eternal potential. It's is difficult to tell that a caterpillar can truly become a butterfly, but we know that with God, all things are possible. Keep the "I am a child of God" attitude in your spirit and believe it. Most important, remember that who you are this moment is a far cry from what you will become.

We feel like caterpillars at times—undeveloped, self-centered, unattractive human souls without hope of transformation. Even when we hear that God's grace is sufficient to redirect our paths, we feel unworthy of His favor. But when we are at our worst, God is at His best. "My grace is sufficient for you, for my power is made perfect in weakness" (2 Corinthians 12:9).

Only when we understand we have no virtues other than those given by God and that left to our own devices we will surely fall, we will be ready to face the most crucial reality in our life. Jesus declares, "Those of you who do not give up everything you have cannot be my disciples" (Luke 14:33). Jesus was talking about surrendering our nests, specifically those things that have become our obsessions. But even when we understand that they are idols and that God requires us to surrender them to make room for Him, like Lot's wife, we cling.

One of my favorite books of inspiration, *Steps to Christ*, offers a striking illustration of the challenges we face when we're confronted with surrendering fully to be consecrated to God.

A cow appeared in the parking lot of a company that serviced airplanes. Several employees tried to herd it to greener pastures, but their uniforms included red shirts. The cow charged, activated an automatic door, and chased one of the employees through the lobby and into the manager's office. The employee escaped through a back door, trapped the cow in the boss's office without appointment, and phoned for help.

The 650-pound cow demolished a coffee table, dented a desk, kicked holes in the walls, and crushed a plant. When help arrived, the uninvited 650-pound guest taxied peaceably out of the office into a trailer.

Sometimes, our attempts to remove idolatry from our lives are only halfhearted, just like wearing a red shirt while trying to shoo a cow away. Before we know it, the Devil has ignored the "Employees Only" sign and is firmly entrenched in our manager's office. If we're serious about it, we must make a total commitment to remove idolatry.[21]

How much is too much to give up for God? He gave up everything for us, so we should hold back nothing; we should live in full compliance with His will.

In *Turn Your Life Around,* Dr. Tim Clinton wrote,

> The good news is that God is always at work to win our hearts. He loves to use our brokenness and powerlessness to send us fleeing back to Him … There is a path to healing if you will cast your eyes on the Lover of your soul. New beginnings start with an understanding of what has happened each step of the way in the downward spiral your natural tendency will be to bypass the effort to understand your pain and instead focus on recovery.[22]

Scars heal, but not overnight. Your adverse nesting experiences can be swept under the carpet and forgotten; that's the easy way out, or come to think of it, no way out at all. But when Jesus' marvelous grace appears, it will start things in motion. The lubricant of forgiveness massages deep into the epidermis and blots out every trace of every scar.

Paul of Tarsus's encounter with Christ on the road to Damascus transformed his destiny and rehabilitated his reputation from murderer to man of God. When God reaches down and offers to turn your mess into your message, don't "kick against the pricks," let Him!

We all are dealing with baggage from dysfunctional nests, including broken hearts, tarnished characters, gunshyness due to failed

---

21 www.whiteestate.org/books/sc/sc7.html

22 Hachette Book Group, Wheaton, Illinois.

relationships, and rattled nerves. But that's not God's desire for our lives—it's not what He created us to be. We're not to hang our heads in that "I'm nobody" mode for the rest of our lives.

If you ever doubt you can be set free, feel the energy from David's experience and how God walked with him in difficult and desperate times. He wants to set you up for the trip of your life! Take one step at a time, and ask God to show you your possibilities; He has a plan for your future even if you find yourself heading into your golden years; you can celebrate every day as a special, precious gift of God.

But even as you celebrate, the Enemy will use individuals to raise up unreasonable standards for you. They will constantly keep your long-ago past held high before your face. His idea is to discourage you from believing you have in fact surrendered your past and are thus a bona fide child of God with all its rights and privileges. But God said, "I am he who blots out your transgressions, for my own sake, and remembers your sins no more" (Isaiah 43:25). So when the Enemy reminds you about your past nest, remind him about his future home. You will be in the clear, so celebrate that. As long as you remain faithful to God and honor Him always, no missile aimed at you will take you down.

We can't change where we came from, but we can affect the environment we create for our kids. As the Beatles wrote, "And in the end, the love you take is equal to the love you make."

A Letter from God Concerning Your Surrender

My little children,

I write to you because I love you. You need to know you are the apple of my eye. More than anything else, I want you to seek me while I may be found. I am never too busy or important that I cannot be available to you. I am the best companion you can ever have.

Even when your days are cloudy and your mind is ill at ease, reach out to me. I know you've been through many seasons, but I am near you now, and I am expecting to meet you at the end of this letter. Just so you don't forget, remember your ragged nest and realize I am in the process of rebuilding it. Have patience, and trust me each day.

Love,

Your Father God

Chapter Four

SHACKING UP IS A FRAUD

Want the Milk? Buy the Whole Cow!

*H*e shamelessly tugged at her heart, slobbering on her face from ear to ear. That was the serpent speaking. That's how he gains access—first the hissing, then the rattling, then the fangs come out. That's lots of forewarning, but things happen so fast when our minds are not focused on God's do nots, and almost imperceptibly the strike!

> The woman said to the serpent, "We may eat fruit from the trees in the garden, but God did say, 'You must not eat fruit from the tree that is in the middle of the garden, and you must not touch it, or you will die.'"
> (Genesis 3:2–4)

Just how did the serpent charm Eve's socks off? We know from the serpent's own words that he had swagger: "You will not surely die," the serpent said to the woman. "For God knows that when you eat of it your eyes will be opened, and you will be like God, knowing good and evil" (Genesis 3:4–5). But was that enough to cause the first mother to disobey God's command? Why did Eve think she had the chutzpah to be equal to God? Adding to or subtracting from God's words creates a dilemma. Robert Deffinbaugh makes a point.

> The fruit of the tree was not good for food because God had forbidden Eve and her husband to eat it. And neither was the fruit of the tree able to make one wise. The tree was able to do what its name indicates. It was not called the "tree of wisdom" but the "tree of knowledge of good and evil.[23]

Three people—Adam, Eve, and the serpent—had different interpretations of God's word but one corporate unwise decision: to sidestep God's commands. Though Eve blamed the serpent for tricking her, she had consciously decided to disobey God.

One word of caution to young people who are considering cohabitating: Don't! The law of God is not in your favor, and neither is the law of the land. I can hear opposing voices: "It's a monogamous relationship, so why not?" "We're getting married anyway." "There is no scripture in the Bible that prohibits shacking up."

But look! You know something isn't sitting well with the idea of shacking up when a very smart eighteen-year-old tells her boyfriend, "Any time you can have free milk without buying the cow, you have a problem. And it's an even more serious problem when the free milk is yours."

Pulling Back the Sheets

Whether because of rebellion, convenience, or blatant disregard for the sacredness of marriage, the statistics are clear—an increasing number of Americans are shacking up. Shacking up is not as innocent as it might seem; it has serious and long-lasting effects on the man and the woman, not to mention any children who might become parts of such relationships.

---

23 "Let Me See Thy Glory," Robert Deffinbaugh, 1997 Biblical Studies Press, LLC and the authors.

Shacking up was once frowned upon and considered a sin, but not so now. Even the phrase *shacking up* is becoming obsolete. Could it be that the status quo is just another experiment that after it runs its course will discover its way back to its start? Did society fall off the cliff, or is there a reasonable explanation for boyfriend and girlfriend to come together and mutually decide to cohabit or "be roommates" as the act is frequently referred to?

David Popenoe and Barbara Defoe in *Divorce Culture* and coauthors of the report in the National Marriage Project "Should We Live Together? What Young Adults Need to Know About Cohabitation Before Marriage," found that there are "clear and present dangers for women and children" in common-law relationships and that such unions endanger the stability of possible marriages. The report noted that "half of all American marriages are preceded by a 'trial marriage,' whereby the couple lives together before exchanging wedding vows." The report found that 60 percent of high school seniors felt that living together before marriage was a good way to "find out whether they [a couple] really get along."

But let's be real—what message does the normalizing of shacking up send our men and women young and old? On the surface, shacking up might seem like a convenient, practical, harmless idea, but the testimonies from young people (particularly younger women) by and large tell a collective tale of regret. For women (particularly younger women), the message might well be that he's the one and if you don't catch him while you can, you might lose out on love forever. For men (particularly younger men), the signal is equally troubling—sow as many wild oats as possible before you move on to the one you want to marry.

Oh what a tangled web we weave when we depart from the instructions of God! It's impossible to engage in a mock marriage without Jesus between your sheets and later on look at the sheets as pure and sacred! God wants to get all up in your business—wise folks understand that purity has its perks, and respecting the marital bed means that because you kept your sheets pure, His will and purpose for this wonderful part of your life will be blessed.

This business of sampling the fruit before purchasing it originated with the first family in the garden of Eden; the result was the fall. Today, such "sampling" before marriage is no less sinister an act. God made the fruit for obedient consumption, so take His word for it—you don't need to sample it. A man who contends he wants a sample is being truthful; what he actually wants is free fruit here, there, everywhere under the guise of looking for the right fruit. Who in the world made him a connoisseur of fruit? Be on the lookout for the professional sampler! Remember Satan's words to Eve: "You shall not surely die." Once you understand the account of the fall, you will appreciate the emotional, social, and spiritual toll disobedience had on Eve and will have on those today who in their rebellion decide to circumvent God's plan for the marital bed by playing house.

> Adam and Eve let themselves believe that eating the forbidden fruit was so small a matter that it could not cause the terrible results that God said would come. But this "small" matter was disobeying God's unchangeable, holy law. Disobedience separated the human family from God and let sorrow and death come into the world. Century after century a never-ending sad cry has gone up from the earth. The whole world is suffering because man disobeyed God. Heaven itself has felt the effects. Christ had to die on Calvary because man broke the divine law. Let us never think of sin as a small thing. Every sin, every turning away from the grace of God, hardens our hearts. It leads us to make wrong choices. It keeps us from understanding God's love. Sin makes us less willing to obey, less able to yield to God's Holy Spirit.[24]

---

24 *Happiness Digest*, 14.

Stop. Look. Listen.

The ride will be amazing. The fun you'll have will far outweigh the guilt. Others do it, and it works out. No matter the consequences, just eat it. You live only once. We'll cross that bridge when we get to it—whenever the conscience is bombarded with these kinds of denials and justifications, the smart thing to do is to stop, look, and listen.

Knowing the Bible's warnings about the consequences of sexual immorality, is any desire no matter how intense worth the risk? Are these consequences the price you want to pay? Maybe the price of a very attractive dress is just too high for you. What do you do? Tuck it in your purse and walk off without paying for it? You know the consequences of shoplifting, so you would exercise self-control and simply walk away.

Years ago, I was a high school debate coach. I held a mock session to get a feel for how well the teams had prepared for a debate. Unbeknownst to me, Dominique, a team leader who was to be first in the actual debate was a staunch proponent of abstinence before marriage and was all fired up to defend her position. Her teammate Walter, on the other hand, held extremely liberal views on the subject; he maintained that it would be foolish not to do "a little sampling" before making a commitment.

"What is your reasoning for changing the rules of the Bible to fit your own standards?" the opposition team contended.

Walt had no immediate response, but energized by what she perceived was a weakness in the other team's stance, Dominique highlighted on the practice board scripture verses to back up her claim: Galatians 5:19, 1 Corinthians 6:9, 1 Corinthians 7:1, Hebrews 13:4, Ephesians 5:5, Ephesians 4:22–24, Romans 12:1, and Ezekiel 16:31.

"Convinced?"

"Don't buy it," Walt avowed.

"Some things are subject to change," Dominique said, "but not God's Word. It stands as is yesterday, today, and forever."

"I'm sticking to my guns," Walt proffered. "After I buy a car, I can't return it, but after I say I do, I can always take her back."

It's been about a decade since I directed that debate program, and times have certainly changed, but so much remains the same, and Bible truths, though snubbed by many, can never be successfully dismissed.

Ladies, you represent the cows with milk, so you're in the driver's seat. Develop your marketing strategies wisely: no samples available—purchase only! Buy the cow or go without milk. If guys talk about taking the car for a test drive, the principle is the same.

If you're still struggling with what to do with the milk and the car, consider this: what's a guy supposed to do with a car when buyer's remorse kicks in and he wants to return it? Sell it as a "used" vehicle for a lesser price? It cannot be stressed enough—you are a "keeper," and you have to believe that! No one will ever know how highly you think of yourself unless you act the part. So heads up, chin up, chest out—you are a child of the King, so that makes you royalty. Royalty never looks or acts cheap, nor does it give samples or discounts!

Don't Crash My Party

The story's told about some broke college students who would present themselves as young professionals and ingratiate themselves to young, unsuspecting female servers at expensive restaurants. They would order pricy dishes, but three quarters of the way through the meal, they would summon the server over and complain about stomach pangs they'd call food poisoning. Other members of the group would also whine about other food-poisoning symptoms; visibly annoyed, they would hurriedly walk out, tab unpaid.

You see this scenario played out over and over again—everything is lovey-dovey as long as the milk is free, but once a demand for payment is made, the setting changes and the "tester" walks out, claiming the vehicle or the cow was not desirable after all.

The analogy of a car and your prized possession is seriously flawed! If he wants to own it, let him put a ring on it. That's how it was back in the day. They courted for a long time (not just dated), and only after an exhaustive examination of the suitor by the girl's matriarch and patriarch was the offer of her hand in marriage accepted. Okay, let's be real—that's all old school, but some old-school stuff is great, and derisively dismissing the wisdom of Grandma and Grandpa will not override their sound teachings.

The more serious issue of what God says is at the heart of the matter: shacking up is not a part of His plan for His children, and any departure from it by shacking up is a step in the wrong direction. The evidence is all too clear: the judicial system is overloaded with heartbreaking stories about stolen innocence in mock marriages.

Yolande (not her real name), a young girl I mentored, is in her early twenties. She moved in with Keith (not his real name) after being smitten with his persona. Currently in counseling, the young woman is severely scarred from her experience of shacking up. This excerpt from Yolanda's journal has been heavily edited.

> There isn't a day that goes by that I don't think about my years with Joe. Many days I struggle—I fight with God. I no, He didn't make me do it, but He should have stopped it from getting so out of hand. Why? Now I'm broken inside and empty. Would they all walk away now? Would they? Part of me is left with him and I will never trust another man with my body—never. Maybe one day I'll get myself back, I hope so, but for now I have to deal with me. Yes, I was fooled—messed over, taken for a ride, a very expensive ride. The pain right now, the emptiness.

Satan's Blueprints

The fingerprints of Satan are all over the concept of "shacking up." Many people enter this union with not much more than ecstasy and raging hormones; in the vast majority of cases, they just as quickly walk away with deep regrets and lifelong scars. And children born in such environments invariably repeat the cycle later. After all, shacking up is not nature influenced, it is nurture (environment) influenced. What message does it send our children? Boys learn that commitment is a fallacy, that it's fine to cut and run at will, and women learn that anything as an alternative to living alone is acceptable, that waiting for marriage belongs to the premodern era. This attitude presupposes that there is no advantage to saving oneself for a permanent relationship, and it also assumes that there are no real consequences to cohabiting or shacking up in truth. "And so the cycle begins ... shack up, move out—shack up, move out, shack up, move out."[25]

We're living in a society in which no one wants to wait for anything. Instant oatmeal may be great on a busy work morning, and one touch of the remote will get you to your favorite news channel, but should the convention and purity of marriage be downgraded to microwaved oats or the touch of the remote control?

In earlier times, dating had one purpose—to help people find mates for life. But bit by bit, one couple at a time, the notion of building a family in the parameters of marriage fell by the wayside; the result is that more and more couples are shacking up, once called living in sin.

Do Good People Shack Up?

Shacking up may seem innocent and in many instances financially and socially convenient, but this knockoff relationship that mimics marriage becomes downright dangerous especially when children are involved

---

25 K. Horatio Pratt, Counseling Psychologist, 2013.

and when the parties involved feeling uncommitted begin hopping from one relationship to another.

I had a matter before the courts a few years ago that dragged on for many months. While I was waiting in court, I had the opportunity to observe just a bit of what happens when couples decide to play house instead of marry. I heard case after case that involved young couples involved in disputes over child support, restraining orders, or domestic violence. One young woman met her boyfriend eight or nine months before the birth of their child. The Petitioner already had a young child from a different relationship, a two-year old daughter. This is the account as best as I remember it.

> This is the fifth time my ex and I have been in court over child support. At the first hearing, I was happy when the judge ordered him to pay $500 a month. Since that time, my ex always in perfect health, has left his corporate job, gone on disability, and filed for bankruptcy. Suspension of license was ineffective, and his younger brother took him in and drove him everywhere he needed to go. Right now, I have nothing—the children are sick and I have no money to take them to the doctor, one of them needs to see a specialist; and I am done!
>
> After today, all that's left is going to a shelter; this thought terrifies me!

The voices I heard and the people I watched in the courtroom led me to ask myself, *What is the emotional cost of shacking up? Why is that cost rarely discussed?*

In an ordinary relationship in which couples live apart, the worst thing that could happen in case of a breakup is a broken heart. Not so with shacking up, for even when there is a clear-cut case before the court, the court is limited in the amount and the kinds of legal remedy it can award.

All those who date, Christians included, should be prepared for this question: "Why don't we just move in together?" What's actually being said is, "Let's do a test drive, and if we don't like it, no harm, no foul." What never comes up is whether the emotional mileage from the test drive of shacking up can ever be regained.

In 2005, the Census Bureau reported 4.85 million cohabiting couples, up more than ten times from 1960, when there were 439,000 such couples. The 2002 National Survey of Family Growth found that more than half of all women ages fifteen to forty-four have lived with an unmarried partner.[26]

This surge in "shacking up" could be viewed in two ways: people, even some who profess relationships with God, want to have their relationships on their own terms, and as a part of that independence, they see nothing wrong with "shacking up" because so many others are doing it, it doesn't hurt anyone else, and they don't feel they can "contain" themselves.

Flip your page back to the story of Eve and remember how the serpent played with her mind: "Did God really say you must not eat from any tree in the garden?" (Genesis 1:1). God never intended for us to play around with the fundamental family structure He had ordained. But here is a teachable moment: God's grace is great enough to cover your sheet mistakes.

> No temptation has seized you except what is common to man. And God is faithful; he will not let you be tempted beyond what you can bear. But when you are tempted, he will also provide a way out so that you can stand up under it. (1 Corinthians 10:13)

Sexual intimacy is an awesome thing given to us by God to enjoy, but it is amazing how a good thing can be used to destroy us.

---

26 Cohabitation in the United States, From Wikipedia, the free encyclopedia" (1) Report: Most Couples Living Together Marry." (2) Cohabitation is replacing dating.

Postscript

I unintentionally used this chapter in a presentation to a single's group when a lovely couple asked, "If you're already living together, what do you do?" Judging by a previous comment this couple had made, I anticipated where they were coming from and answered, "Get out! There's nothing to argue about—get out, because the longer you look at your stack of sheet violations, the easier it is to become discouraged, and when you become discouraged, the easier it is to justify making a spiritual decision."

Chapter Five
Finding Mr. Right: Stuff Nobody Told Me!

Delight yourself in the LORD and he will
give you the desires of your heart.
—Psalm 37:4

When your feet hit the floor when you rise in the mornings
praise God for not having the wrong person in your life!

A young lady who is pure will shine with radiance in a world
of utter chaos where everything seems to be falling apart.

One organization says it can help you find Mr. Right in ninety-five days; one says it can help you find Mr. Right in sixty days, and another organization says it will take only thirty days. Book after book is written on the subject of finding Mr. Right, and many of them are on the best seller list, but has anyone ever really found Mr. Right? Dig a little deeper with me to see if we can uncover the true identity of this elusive guy.

In Nora Ephron's romantic comedy *When Harry Met Sally*, Harry self-righteously asserts that men and women can never be friends. Sally passionately disagrees. Though the point is made in a lighthearted and comedic way, one lesson comes through: relationships take time, and lasting relationships require among other things friendship first.

Do you really want to get behind the wheel of a car before learning to drive? So is it with getting to know someone with the expectations of a long-term relationship—it's a serious undertaking. It will not be an overreach to draw an analogy here with piloting an airplane. A pilot must go through a lot of training, preparation on the flight deck, safety checks, closing the cabin door, safety briefing, pushing back, and taxiing all before takeoff. Imagine a pilot trying all that without a checklist! Just as pilots have to follow protocol prior to takeoff, so too is it important to advance a relationship only after the necessary steps are followed: platonic friendship (without benefits), close friendship, and special friendship.

It may not be a bad idea to dream about your wedding day and Stevie Wonder's song *Ribbon in the Sky* playing, but understand that the wedding day is one of the happiest yet most serious occasions. After the honeymoon, then what? If you've stayed in step with the Spirit and listened to the voice of God, you should be on solid footing.

When my blood brother found out I was writing this book and was interested in including a chapter on how to find Mr. Right, he sent me a testimonial that outlined some of the ingredients in his relationship that had made his marriage last for half a century. One of his points that jumped out at me was, "Just because someone is not the right match for you doesn't mean he [or she] is not the right match for someone else." This statement presupposed that a single should not go on a campaign to find Mr. Right. True, as normal people, each of us at some point in our lives are attracted to another being. Great! At last there's a connection. The problem arises, however, when too much pressure is put on the other individual as the single lady who darts into the new relationship with premature expectation of marriage rather than allowing God to lead as hopefully the friendship takes off.

Permit me to share the precious pearls my brother wrote about looking for Mr. Right.

> Look at your fingers. Did you notice that they're of different sizes? Think about your search for Mr. Right as a marathon with numerous runners. Though they might all finish, only one will win. Life is often like your uneven fingers, and waiting on God to act in your individual circumstances as you wait for Mr. Right demands patience and endurance. I waited for thirty-three years; my wait wasn't always easy but it was always accepted. I saw friends of mine walk down the aisle to receive the woman of their dreams; actually, I was best man at a few of their weddings. I asked why not me on a few occasions. I even watched the girl of my dream pull away and give her heart to someone else. But each time I was rebuffed, each time I participated in a wedding, my faith was oddly enough strengthened.
>
> Some of the promises you learn early stick with you, such as Jeremiah 31:3: "The Lord appeared to us in the past, saying: I have loved you with an everlasting love; I have drawn you with unfailing kindness," or Psalm 37:4, "Take delight in the Lord, and he will give you the desires of your heart."
>
> I am not embarrassed to say that looking back, I was not quite ready for marriage anyway, and today, I thank God for helping me to wait and not force a situation. There were lots of kinks in my childhood that needed to be straightened out before I could venture into that sacred phase of my life. God kept working on me, and I believed that as long as He was on the job, that meant He was not finished with me. So what's my testimony? Five words: "In the fullness of time …" I'm

on record: thirty-three years, one wife (the love of my
life), three beautiful children, three grandchildren, and
an incredible marriage!

I stumbled across this blog recently: God's Assurance/My Utmost for
His Highest utmost.org/god's-assurance/Jun 5, 2013 and I thought I'd
send you the link. I was immediately drawn to this excerpt: "Have we
learned to sing after hearing God's keynote? Are we continually filled
with enough courage to say, "The Lord is my helper"?

It would not surprise me to know that you are at a crossroad trying to
decide on whether to throw caution to the wind and step outside of
God's will for your life. You have waited long enough you think, and
still no Mr. Right. May I encourage you that the darkest hour is always
just before dawn? Ride out your lonely nights with songs of God's
promise that He will never leave you nor forsake you, that He will
keep your heart and mind pure until the appointed sheet time. "And
the peace of God, which transcends all understanding, will guard your
hearts and your minds in Christ Jesus" (Philippians 4:7).

Chapter Six

GUARDING THE AVENUES OF THE HEART

Above all else, guard your heart, for everything you do flows from it.
—PROVERBS 4:23

Caution—Do Not Enter

*I*f there were no safeguards in place to filter harmful contaminants, we would ingest destructive bacteria. When we refuse to guard our senses, the gateways to our hearts, we run the risk of being invaded by the Enemy. Have you not understood that the Lord God desires you to guard your mind lest Satan gain control over it? Take heed lest while you are operating with your guard down, Satan is canvassing the territory for a chance to turn your thoughts away from God.

There's real danger in thinking that because we are mature Christian we are therefore exempt from entrapment from the Enemy. Every Christian must guard every nook and cranny of his or her soul lest a breach of security gives the Enemy access.

Is it impossible to control our sexual desires? Yes and no. We have sinful natures, so we'll continue to struggle with sin. That's why we need a Savior.

> We do not have a high priest who is unable to sympathize with our weaknesses, but we have one who has been tempted in every way, just as we are—yet was without sin. (Hebrews 4:15–16)

But here is some good news: Satan cannot enter the mind without our consent.

It is easy for "seekers" to become discouraged believing that guarding the avenues of the heart is impossible. But we should remember God expressly said,

> No temptation has overtaken you except what is common to mankind. And God is faithful; he will not let you be tempted beyond what you can bear. But when you are tempted he will also provide a way out so that you can endure it. (1 Corinthians 10:13)

So what do we say to the seeker looking on from the outside? We say the struggle with sin is natural. We were born in sin and formed in iniquity, so we need a Savior, just as Paul wrote above.

The clarion call is to honor God in your singleness. Society has strayed a long way from the days when the marriage bed was a symbol of honor and fresh beginnings. And unless society could demonstrate that the breakdown in marriage and family and an inarguably gross disrespect for law and order have directly impacted the state of our nations today, then therein lies much of our problem.

If you're addicted to shows like *Sex in the City*, the *Jerry Springer Show*, or *Scandal*, consider checking your moral compass. What business do Christians have enjoying dramas built on deceit and betrayal that glamorize cheating and applaud infidelity in marriage?

I first encountered the phrase "garbage in, garbage out" (GIGO) in a computer class years ago. The instructor made sure the phrase stuck in our minds. If tainted data gets into a computer, the computer will produce tainted results. When I think about the importance of protecting my heart from contaminants, GIGO becomes relevant. Whatever our minds feed on is what we will become. When junk food is continually ingested, it will corrupt our bodies. Paul could have been thinking about GIGO when he wrote, "But among you there must not be even a hint of sexual immorality, or of any kind of impurity, or of greed, because these are improper for God's holy people" (Ephesians 5:3). James 1:14–16 tells us,

> But each person is tempted when they are dragged away by their own evil desire and enticed. Then, after desire has conceived, it gives birth to sin; and sin, when it is full-grown, gives birth to death. Don't be deceived, my dear brothers and sisters.

Sin Begins in the Mind

What does it mean for Christians to guard their hearts? Does it mean they cannot date or have any interaction with the opposite sex? No. But when it comes to guarding their hearts, they will likewise establish ways to make sure they're not exposed to the Enemy's attacks. If Christians ever see a lion lurking in the backyard, they know it's not looking for a place to have a Bible study; they know it's looking for prey. "Be alert and of sober mind. Your enemy the devil prowls around like a roaring lion looking for someone to devour" (1 Peter 5:8).

Dangers of Overconfidence

Pro sports talent will tell you that one of the greatest challenges to winning is overconfidence. I watched a 2012 basketball game between the Miami Heat and the Washington Wizards, perhaps my most stressful yet. The Miami Heat appeared to be strutting, exuding overconfidence, when the Wizards (NBA's worst team), obviously sensing what some commentators subsequently called "Heat arrogance," stepped up their game and eked out a 105–101 win.

Confidence is a prerequisite for winning, but God warns us of spiritual overconfidence. He wants us to always remain connected to the Vine, for we are most vulnerable when we are at our strongest. That's precisely why the apostle Paul wrote, "So, if you think you are standing firm, be careful that you don't fall!" (1 Corinthians 10:12). One game does not a season make; yesterday's spiritual success doesn't guarantee tomorrow's. Guarding the avenues of the heart requires daily surrendering to God, for it is only when we continually acknowledge our human vulnerability that we will start relying daily on God's grace.

Mark 14:38 should inspire us to remain attached to the Vine both in season and out of season: "Watch and pray so that you will not fall into temptation. The spirit is willing, but the flesh is weak."

"It is not in my own strength and worthiness I come, Father, but out of a deep conviction of my own fleshly vulnerability. I realize that it's only because of Your grace and mercy that I could stand clean and pure … purge me even now with hyssop and make me clean—wash me and I will be whiter than snow, then help me to submit myself daily for fresh examination and anointing. It is in you and you alone that I live and move and have my being. Thank you, Father, for keeping my life clean, and may I forever be kept to the utmost. Amen!"

So you're not hooked up and everyone else is. Christmas parties, banquets, weddings—all special occasions attended by couples! When the pressure's on, that's when you need a solid support system. Hopefully you can find it in your parents or some trusted partner who has walked that road before to counsel and encourage you to accept your singleness as a precious gift from God. Understand that the choice of a soul mate is not a trivial but a divine matter, so your approach to that must be directed by your Creator. You need a personal, intimate relationship with God to guide you through this important stage.

If your relationship with God is weak or nonexistent, don't take another step before you rectify that! You need God to guide you in what are the most serious deliberations of your life. No matter how difficult it is to contain your sexual desires, don't settle for less than God's best. He wants you to remember He is always writing your story; whatever doesn't fit in His agenda won't fit in yours.

God knows your human frailties and the importance of companionship in your life, but He doesn't want you to be simply "hooked up" with a mate; He wants you to be wholly joined to your mate in a harmonious relationship He can bless. God is on your side; whatever society portrays, God wants you to have unspeakable joy. "For I know the plans I have for you, declares the Lord, plans to prosper you and not to harm you, plans to give you hope and a future" (Jeremiah 29:11).

Chapter Seven

WHEN YOUR DESIRES AND GOD'S WILL CLASH

Therefore God gave them over in the sinful desires of their hearts to sexual impurity for the degrading of their bodies with one another.
—ROMANS 1:24

Collisions happen when two or more things come together violently. What happens when our desires and God's will collide? Indeed, there are times when God's will for our lives is a far cry from what we feel is best for us. We instantly start digging in. "I want what I want and I want it now!" "I'll go off on my own and bring God in the picture later!" It's a collision of wills. Our desires might seem reasonable and straightforward at first, but how can we determine for a fact what God's will is for us? We're bombarded by multiple voices making convincing claims, so how can we know which one is the voice of God and which is the voice of the Enemy?

Even if we have a right relationship with God, doubts about who's speaking will haunt us at times, and that's intimidating. How can we tell? Here's a help: God will never deal harshly with you when leading you in the right path. His voice is still and calm, never aggressive or agitated. The Enemy on the other hand closes in like a desperate salesman—"My way or the highway!"

I needed to hear from God at a critical time in my life when I had to make a decision about sending my daughter, who wasn't quite sixteen, to college. What do you do with a child prodigy who graduates high school nearly three years early? Could she safely navigate her way socially and successfully through college in a foreign country away from family and friends? My fears were real; my doubts were even more profound. I listened to the conflicting advice from my pastoral people, but I still needed more—I wanted to know for myself up close and personal what God wanted me to do, so I went into a season of prayer and fasting. That was when for the first time I realized God responds with unambiguity. What settled peace overwhelmed me! I ended up having no doubts that sending my daughter to college at such a tender age was in accordance with God's will.

Jesus said in John 10:27, "My sheep listen to my voice; I know them, and they follow me." Paul wrote in 1 Corinthians 14:33, "God is not the author of confusion."

> The God who loved you enough to die for you loves you enough to talk to you. And wherever you are in your spiritual walk, God will find a way to speak to you in a way you will understand.[27]

So some voice tells you that you've been on the market for some time, girlfriend after girlfriend has tied the knot, but you're all alone in the corner at a party. Your heart tells you to obey God, but your head spars with your heart and tells you that if you continue to hold out, life will pass you by. That's a monumental collision! But the same God who is evident in the bowing down of the trees and in the gusting of the wind is the same God who invites you to rely on Hebrews 13:5: "Never will I leave you; never will I forsake you." Hold on to that assurance; believe

---

27   Priscilla Schirer, *Discerning the Voice of God: how to Recognize When God Speaks.*

that before God can do a great work in and through you, your spiritual conflicts have to be resolved and your selfish desires must be tamed.

The warfare against self is the greatest battle ever. The yielding of self, the surrendering of all to the will of God is a struggle, but the soul must submit to God before it can be renewed in holiness.[28] What White seems to be affirming was Paul's statement in Romans 8:7: "The mind governed by the flesh is hostile to God; it does not submit to God's law, nor can it do so."

Our struggle is not in determining God's will because we pretty much know what He requires of us. Our battle is with our unregenerate lives. We are continually searching for options, but the more we search, the more we discover we live to please God or to please our flesh.

Paul would cosign Eugene Peterson's point I mentioned earlier about making a dog into a person. Actually, he used the phrase "thorn in my flesh" to describe the temptations that dogged his mind and impeded his walk with God. He pleaded to God to remove them. Whether or not God will always remove our sexual challenges when we pray as Paul did is suspect; perhaps the more appropriate route would be to ask God to help us effectively deal with our temptations. Nevertheless, God responded to Paul's request, "My grace is sufficient for you, for my power is made perfect in weakness" (2 Corinthians 12:7). David wrote in Psalm 34:18, "The Lord is close to the brokenhearted and saves those who are crushed in spirit."

David's assurance to stand by us during our hour of temptation when our faith is weak and our flesh is strong signals that we should trust and never doubt. If God has told us He has a bundle of blessing for us, why would we ever discount His word and allow disbelief to factor Him out of the equation? If He has told us He will make our sheets fulfilled, why should we ever rush into questionable situations?

But why the delay? That question pops up when things aren't going our way or not moving as fast as we'd like. God is not like a microwave

---

28 www.gilead.net/egw/books/misc/Steps_to_Christ/5_Consecration

or a fast-food drive-through, nor can we refresh Him as we do our computers when they're slow. How would we learn obedience, patience, and appreciation and build our characters if God jumped every time we made demands of Him? We'd be spiritual dwarfs, and He wouldn't be God. He uses our waiting to develop us into unwavering men and women.

But if waiting on God always seems easy, it's not—partial obedience is! Half-obedience is not obedience at all in the eyes of God, and that's why God didn't accept Cain's sacrifice. Cain knew what an acceptable offering was, but he used his reasoning and his own ways with the sacrifice rather than obedience.

The story of God's rejection of Cain's sacrifice is a poignant lesson for those who desire to obey God. It demonstrates that partial obedience is still disobedience, and its results are horrifying. Look to our first parents in Genesis 1 to figure out that God expects total loyalty from those who would follow Him.

> After Adam and Eve had eaten of the forbidden fruit, they were filled with a sense of shame and terror. At first their only thought was how to excuse their sin and escape the dreaded sentence of death. Hence the Lord inquired concerning their sin, Adam replied, laying the guilt partly upon God and partly upon his companion.[29]

The story of Lot's wife in Genesis 19 reaffirms the incredible lessons learned from Adam and Eve's disobedience in Genesis 1. She tried to survive on a shoestring of faith in God. At first glance, Lot's wife's behavior was not as startling, since in the beginning, she was apparently willing to heed God's instructions. But somewhere in this woman's thinking things through, her love for the world superseded her love for God. "Remember Lot's wife," said Jesus. The warning couldn't be more pressing; that woman's story is a teachable moment.

---

29   White, Steps to Christ, Youth Edition, and p. 40, Review & Herald Publishing Association.

What was her desire? What was God's will for her? We cannot read her heart—only God could—but we know that at some point, she found herself torn between what she knew to be right and an unsatisfied past. She "started" the journey, but unsettled belief came up, and taking just a few steps on the journey didn't cut it. God wants us to follow His will without qualification or equivocation. It's one thing to start the journey but quite another to finish it and receive the reward. The choice to forego carnal desires in favor of God's will is choice that must be settled in favor of total obedience to God.

A Sense of Purpose

Learn a lesson on single-mindedness from a successful marathon runner who doesn't focus on the total mileage but more so on the joys ahead. The roadblocks of psychological pressures, pain, opposition jitters, and the possibility of failure are real and could seriously impact the chances of success. What were the challenges Lot's wife faced? Did she clearly understand God's will? Even if she didn't, should she have accepted it at face value? We are left to wonder whether she had a grief-stricken heart over lost family and friends or a silly heart that desired the abundance of material wealth she left behind.

Joe Crews wrote,

> The society there was shameless, degenerate, and entirely sex-perverted. Mrs. Lot not only moved into Sodom, but Sodom moved into her. She was the type who loved fine things, and the mad whirl of social activities fascinated her from the beginning. She was soon caught up in the excitement of party rounds of pleasure, and the evidence seems to indicate that she eventually shared much of the materialistic mind-set of the Sodomites.[30]

---

30 www.amazingfacts.org/media-library/book/e/.../remember-lots-wife.aspx

The essence of Crew's statement is sober: Lot's wife's home, friends, and all the niceties she was leaving behind must have been more important to her than total obedience to God. We still find many people exactly like her. They also believe the truth, know what they ought to do, and want to be saved. They linger just as she did, waiting until the pull of the world overpowers their will to act, and they are not able to let go of things. She looked back and was turned into a pillar of salt. Lot and his wife never got to realize what blessings God had for them.

When we replace God's will with our own, we risk missing out on blessings earmarked specifically by God for us. Lot's story is a lesson for us: we must resist our pleasures even if they don't seem inherently inappropriate; that's not what is important in the scheme of things. Even if our intent is noble, even if it's reasonable, if it's outside God's individualized plan for us, we must ignore it in favor of God's agenda. It is only as we "die" every day immersed in God's perfect will that we will be in harmony with God. "Remember Lot's wife" (Luke 17:32). Her account serves as a perpetual warning against our trying to make adjustments to God's plan; we must accept His will at face value.

> There is no blueprint—any certain way of knowing the Will of God in our material decisions. Our God-given intellect and the discernment of His Spirit living in our hearts, will give us the necessary tools to make better than average correct decisions. Sometimes His permitting will allow our failures to exercise our Faith, increase our Hope and cause us to cling to Him as our Friend in need.[31]

We can never regulate our desire to indulge in sexual sins without the help of God. Good intentions will not suffice, nor will fine upbringings. Professionals can offer little if any relief. Our spirits may be willing but our flesh will always be weak; however, the giants in our lives cannot compare to the power of Christ. When we find ourselves trying

---

31 (Two Wills, His and Mine), Mother M. Angelica. www.ewtn.com/library/mother/ma2wills.htm

but failing, trying again but failing again, it's time to let God do the unthinkable for us. He can!

> As always, Jesus is our pattern. Doing God's will was food for his soul: "My food is to do the will of Him who sent me and to accomplish His work" (John 4:34). He plainly stated, "I do not seek my own will, but the will of Him who sent me" (John 5:30; cf. 6:38–40). When we live as Jesus lived—for the will of God—then we experience a kinship with Jesus. We share the same passion, the same heart, the same mission, for we serve the same purpose—the manifestation of the kingdom of God by living God's will. Right here. Right now. In big decisions, but mostly in the small ones that make up the bulk of our daily lives.[32]

When faithfulness to God is the focus of our lives, our nature that is submissive to God will transcend our carnal nature thus making it possible to yield to God's will for our lives.

> Those who become new creatures in Christ Jesus will bring forth the fruits of the Spirit, "love, joy, peace, long-suffering, gentleness, goodness, faith, meekness, temperance." Galatians 5:22, 23. They will no longer fashion themselves according to the former lusts but by the faith of the Son of God they will follow in His steps, reflect His character, and purify themselves even as He is pure. The things they once hated they now love, and the things they once loved they hate. The proud and self-assertive become meek and lowly in heart. The vain and supercilious become serious and unobtrusive. The drunken become sober, and the profligate pure. The vain customs and fashions of the world are laid aside. Christians will seek not the "outward adorning," but "the hidden man of

---

32 Ibid.

[p. 59] the heart, in that which is not corruptible, even the ornament of a meek and quiet spirit."[33]

To Everything a Season

Wherever "season" we find ourselves, whether paired up, single, or married, we must find purpose in that season by making God's will a way of life. We must not be presumptuous and disobey because we want something else at the time. Too many people justify running ahead of God; they claim that things were not moving fast enough and that the details were too difficult or not moving in the direction they wanted. Those who interfere with God's plans will spend the future regretting their impatience. They will have lost valuable time, and their relationship with God will have dwindled rather than grown.

You will have opportunities in life that will call on you to choose to defer to God's will for your life or to yield to your fleshly desires. When you do, do not conform to the pattern of this world but be transformed by the renewing of your mind. Then you will be able to test and approve God's good, pleasing, and perfect will (Romans 12:2). For any decision that is made outside the will of God is of no avail and will eventually fail. Whether we want to yield to our desires or not, this does not absolve us from Christ's mandate to not do so. If you're tempted to ask, "If God gives me the desires of my heart, why am I still single?" find your answer in Psalm 37:5–7.

> Trust in the LORD and do good; dwell in the land and enjoy safe pasture. Take delight in the Lord, and he will give you the desires of your heart. Commit your way to the Lord; trust in him and he will do this. Be still before the Lord and wait patiently for him.

When you struggle to remain in God's will, remind yourself of these ten guaranteed promises.

---

33   1 Peter 3:3–4. *Steps to Christ*, 58–59, www.whiteestate.org/books/sc/sc7.htm.

» "The righteous cry out, and the LORD hears them; he delivers them from all their troubles" (Psalm 37:5–7).

"When you pass through the waters, I will be with you; and when you pass through the rivers, they will not sweep over you. When you walk through the fire you will not be burned; the flames will not set you ablaze" (Isaiah 43:2).

» "Know that the Lord has set apart his faithful servant for himself; and the Lord hears when I call to him" (Psalm 4:3).

» "He guides the humble in what is right and teaches them his way" (Psalm 25:9).

» "I am the LORD your God, who brought you up out of Egypt. Open wide your mouth and I will fill it" (Psalm 81:10).

» "He refreshes my soul. He guides me along the right paths for his name's sake" (Psalm 23:3).

» "Wait for the LORD; be strong and take heart and wait for the LORD" (Psalm 27:14).

» "Yet the Lord longs to be gracious to you; therefore he will rise up to show you compassion. For the Lord is a God of justice. Blessed are all who wait for him!" (Isaiah 30:18).

» "No weapon forged against you will prevail, and you will refute every tongue that accuses you. This is the heritage of the servants of the Lord, and this is their vindication from me, declares the Lord" (Isaiah 54:17).

» "He put a new song in my mouth, a hymn of praise to our God. Many will see and fear the LORD and put their trust in him" (Psalm 40:3).

Even if you've tried and failed repeatedly, that's a good thing, because your failures are God's opportunities to bring you into alignment with His will. Isn't it time to let God do the unthinkable for you? He can!

Chapter Eight

SHEETS SECRETS: WWJD?

Be alert and of sober mind. Your enemy the devil prowls around like a roaring lion looking for someone to devour.
—1 PETER 5:8

*I*f Jesus Christ is front and center of your life, then He will be front and center of everything you do—He will be present everywhere you go, and as you tread cautiously and prayerfully in choosing a lifetime partner, He will accompany you in your most intimate moments, even as you contemplate getting between the sheets! And if He is protecting your sheets, nothing or no one that's forbidden will nest there.

Stepping Out in Faith

So you're ready to date? Be aware of one critical bit of information: the kind of relationship you build during your courtship will determine the kind of marriage you will have, the kind of children you will raise, and the kind of future you will carve out for yourself. To Christians, dating ought to offer a bird's-eye view of what a marriage will be.

Because it's difficult to see clearly when love fogs your eyes, what's on your fantasy wish list might very well collide with God's plan for you, so don't be giddy over good looks and other seductive exteriors; look first for exemplary character. A handsome face will weaken at some point. That buffed chest will eventually wilt like flowers in the sun, but inner character will remain. Rather, pursue God's plan for your life with passion and focus because what He offers you will never disappoint—His love will deliver ultimate satisfaction.

When you realize God has already factored you into His divine design, you need not desperately pursue *eros* love, the sexual kind that's subject to change, "for every good and perfect gift is from above, coming down from the Father of the heavenly lights, who does not change like shifting shadows" (James 1:17). It's good news that God is crazy in love with you and that He sacrificed His only Son to guarantee that in Him you will be complete with joy, peace, and lasting love. Who could compete with that?

All That Glitters Is Not Gold

Examine what you are opening yourself up to when you hobnob with the popular, worldly folks who barhop, watch porn, smoke pot, and swap spouses, because that will damage your soul and conscience. Those behaviors are Satan's charms—goods marked up but then discounted to make them look like great deals. They're so superficial—in the absence of a personal relationship with God, no deal is a bargain, and living large outside the protection of Christ will lead to horrifying nightmares. I know this, and I wish someone had told me! What will it profit you to win the trophy only to discover what it's made from shines at a distance but smudges at the first touch?

BOLO—be on the lookout—and zealously guard your soul. God wants the best for you; He is desperate to protect your intimate life from any suffering. Whom you pair up with will either put a smile on God's face or bring Him grief. Do not be yoked to nonbelievers, and do not surrender your dignity and integrity for a morsel of good times. "For what do righteousness and wickedness have in common? Or what fellowship can light have with darkness?" (2 Corinthians 6:14). Paul's counsel begs the million-dollar question: Why do we waste valuable time indulging in debasing things we know will sooner or later affect our focus on God? Paul cautioned, "Therefore come out from them and be separate, says the Lord" (2 Corinthians 6:17).

Paul was spot-on. While someone special can bring abundant bliss to your life, nothing will ever top or replace the love God has for you or the plans He has for your eternal future, so why would you choose to comingle your heart with someone with wobbly spiritual footing?

Many are the stories about couples who, when dating, feel that including God in their affairs is unromantic and archaic, thus they unwisely replace Him in the early stages of their relationship with the other, whom they see as special, wealthy, or affectionate. Whether someone is rich in material or affection, there is great danger in stepping high, feeling full with no need for God, not understanding that you cannot be good without God. You can do good works, but to be fulfilled, your heart must be spiritually altered by Him. "You say, I am rich; I have acquired wealth and do not need a thing. But you do not realize that you are wretched, pitiful, poor, blind and naked?" (Revelation 3:17).

What happens when a relationship settles in and becomes static? That's when couples realize their need for someone to lean on. Sadly, however, they discover that without spiritual nutrients, relationships not centered on God cannot survive the drought phase once real-world challenges emerge. We were warned, "You shall have no other gods before me" (Exodus 20:3). There is only one God, and any other relationship we enter into must never replace Him! Nothing must substitute for God; He will not compete with anyone else. He wants the best for you. "Love that becomes a god becomes a demon," wrote C. S. Lewis.

We can do better!

Does the Christian lady want a relationship, or does she want a fling? At a time when movies and TV shows such as *The Forty-Year-Old Virgin*,

Knocked Up, Made of Honor, Honey Boo Boo, and *Jersey Shore* are so popular, an authentic minority dare to stand against the glamorization of immorality. Some observers believe that glorifying of sex outside marriage, though now a blight on families and society, will eventually diminish and there will be a return to a semblance of core values. Others are convinced our society's moral deterioration has not reached its peak so we should brace ourselves for devastating fallout. Still others believe that society's values are simply evolving, not deteriorating.

Moral standards have eroded, but that does not mean this has been sanctioned by God. It does not mean that because sex outside marriage is an everyday routine, such secular boldness is condoned by God. Who made society the guardian of morality? God has not changed, nor has His plan for us to enjoy the bliss and gratification of intimacy in the bounds of marriage. "Heaven and earth will pass away, but my words will never pass away" (Matthew 24:35). "Marriage should be honored by all, and the marriage bed kept pure, for God will judge the adulterer and all the sexually immoral" (Hebrews 13:4).

When Eve decided to make her will superior to God's will (Genesis 3), she found herself in a shocking predicament that started a downward spiral. She danced with the serpent, the Devil, who softened her with his interpretation of God's clear instructions: "Did God really say you must not eat from any tree in the garden?" How much clearer could God have made his instructions to Eve? Thou shall not mean thou shall not—period!

The Annual Council of the General Conference of SDA wrote,

> It is Satan's purpose to pervert every good thing; and the perversion of the best inevitably leads to that which is worst. Under the influence of passion unrestrained by moral and religious principle, the association of the sexes has, to a deeply disturbing extent, degenerated into license and abuse which results in bondage.[34]

---

34 Annual Council of The General Conference of SDA session in Washington, DC, October 12, 1987.

Even if society is clueless, researchers get it! The evidence of a morally declining society is overwhelming, but rather than sounding the alarm, society seems determined to ignore this reality. In a fairy-tale world, maybe Red Riding Hood could have escaped the Big Bad Wolf if she had stripped for him. Real life, however, is not a fairy tale; when society's basic structures are eaten up by questionable social norms, when God is habitually absent from weighty decision making, the lack of spiritual accountability becomes sobering. Live in the moment! If it feels good, do it! Everybody's doing it! No big deal! Nobody's perfect! These are all voices from the pit of hell. Disobedience comes with a heavy price, and that's why God is calling His people from lives of debauchery to lives of obedience; only then can society change.

> If my people, who are called by my name, will humble themselves and pray and seek my face and turn from their wicked ways, then I will hear from heaven, and I will forgive their sin and will heal their land. (2 Chronicles 7:14)

Whenever you succumb to Satan's "Just a little bit" or "Everybody's doing it" lines, know that he has just mugged you and that nothing is ever short term with him. He wines and dines you in the most luxurious places, and once he gets you to surrender your integrity, he leaves you to wallow in your emptiness. The Enemy's work is meticulously crafted and carefully designed to start you on that downward spiral toward destruction. "Above all else, guard your heart, for everything you do flows from it" (Proverbs 4:23).

Chapter Nine

VOICES FROM THE BIOLOGICAL CLOCK

I tick, I tick, I tick …
But nothing seems to click!
I tick, I tick, I tick …

The LORD makes firm the steps of the one who delights in him; though he
may stumble, he will not fall, for the LORD upholds him with his hand.
—PSALM 37:23–24

When your biological clock begins to cry out in the wee hours of the morning, how do you respond, particularly when you know the wombs of those who live wickedly are seemingly blessed? It is not by accident that David's declaration in Psalm 37 found its way into the sacred pages. If you find yourself stumbling in your impatience with God, wait expectantly for God's answer. Whether that answer is slow or sudden, waiting will be endurable when your heart is humbled with obedience and faith.

We are God's earthen vessels. When God seems unresponsive to our physical needs, we sometimes think He is an absentee father who has spurned his visitation rights and is missing in action. By extension, we think that if God doesn't set things in place for a child to conceive in our wombs, He has somehow lost his relevance and we have missed the mark. This is the voice of the enemy, and you have the power to turn it off at the flip of a switch! God says, "I'm taking you where I want you to be, and in my time I will do for you that which I desire."

Several years ago, my best friend, a devout Christian, slumped into a dark period of despondency when at thirty-five she found herself unhooked. Because she was a committed follower of Christ, fair, lovely, and well educated, she was puzzled that the one thing she desired most was the one thing God "kept" from her. She thought, *Why is falling in love so elusive? Why is my chance of having a child fading when I have so much to offer?* Though such questions are understandable, there's danger in trying to answer all of life's "what ifs." Flying in the face of God and questioning Him does no good. We often shrivel up when in our weakness we cannot understand what God is doing in the grand scheme of things. When we're feeling blessed and the world is rosy, that's when we feel that we're anchored in Christ, that nothing could shake us. But could it be that only when our faith is tested can we really know what stuff we're made of? So what do we do when we can't trace God's hand? We trust His heart. The great psalmist David wrote, "Trust in the Lord and do good; dwell in the land and enjoy safe pasture. Take delight in the Lord, and he will give you the desires of your heart." (Psalm 37:3–5). Good news, isn't it?

David's counsel brings to mind a lady named Rachael who did not have a waiting heart. She became jealous when her sister had children but she did not. Rachel told Jacob, "Give me children or I'll die!" Jacob became angry. "Am I in the place of God, who has kept you from having children?" (Genesis 30:1–2).

It's noteworthy that Rachael in her disappointment cried out to Jacob rather than to God. Even if she had cried out to God, was there a guarantee God would have made her fertile? What message does this send to our women of child-bearing age whose hopes are fast fading, whose biological clocks are ticking away? Don't turn away from God just because your Christmas gift wasn't what you wanted. You asked for a baby and you got a puppy ...

What if God in His wisdom decides it is in your best interests to remain single and childless? The question is important—if you are preoccupied with having a child at any cost, you hopefully would have understood that this is arguably one of the most important decisions you will make in your life, so it would be ill-advised to take on such a task without divine guidance. You must know without a doubt what God's will is for your life to be on solid ground. If you don't understand His plans for you, you will be vulnerable to all the hype and negative pressure around you.

What if your singleness and barrenness have been divinely designed so you may point others to a full knowledge of Jesus Christ? This is why we can't succumb to worldly pressures or become frustrated over our biological clocks. According to everything Christ has left us with on the subject of faith and trust, our biological clocks should not signal when we should have children; that decision is something that should be left up to God.

Seek God's will for your life and believe that He alone knows the beginning from the end and is in control of your biological clock. "'For I know the plans I have for you,'" declares the LORD, "'plans to prosper you and not to harm you, plans to give you hope and a future'" (Jeremiah 29:11). What is that future Jeremiah spoke about as it pertains to your child-bearing status? Could it be that after God has carefully considered your future, He has decided against your wish to birth a child? Paul wrote in Romans 8:28, "And we know that in all things God works for the good of those who love him, who have been called according to his purpose." The rapid ticking of the biological clock in no way means childless women should become desperate because desperation leads to cheap love, which leads to lives of horror.

Refer again to the story of Rachael and Leah in Genesis 29:25 to be encouraged in your trust in God. Several vital lessons there teach us that

God's ways are not ours, nor is His manner of doing things always in sync with what we envision. We must learn to be content with our lot in life, for even those around us we think are living perfect lives wrestle with all sorts of problems.

We learn several things from Leah's life. First, we learn we shouldn't look to anybody else for our happiness. People can disappoint us, and our lives might not turn out the way we dream. We learn we shouldn't compare our lives to those of others. In 2 Corinthians 10:12, we read that those who "compare themselves among themselves, are not wise." Although Leah envied her sister Rachael (because Jacob loved her more), Rachael envied Leah because she had more children. If we learn from Leah and learn to praise God anyway, we will find more contentedness in God than with the things of the world.

Finally, we learn that though it's natural to be afraid when we cannot fathom how God is working, we must trust His hand. Mary was afraid when the angel visited her with the news she would bear a son. Though she knew she had kept herself pure and had done no wrong, she found herself in a quandary: "But the angel said to her, do not be afraid, Mary; you have found favor with God. You will conceive and give birth to a son, and you are to call him Jesus" (Luke 1:30). When our human frailty tries to take hold of us, we need to remember that God is always working on our behalf—He alone is God!

Leah Learns to Be Content

After a while, Leah figured that Jacob would never love her the way he loved her sister. She decided to name her fourth son Judah, meaning "praise." Despite her circumstances, Leah decided to praise the Lord (Genesis 29:35). Although Leah wasn't living the life of her dreams, she had received blessings. She learned to be content and to praise God. More than a thousand years later, Paul learned the same thing: "I have learned in whatever state I am, to be content" he wrote from jail (Philippians 4:11).

Being Leah probably wasn't easy; Rachael was well favored (Genesis 29:17). Perhaps Rachael had all the friends. Maybe Leah thought she would never get married. The Bible doesn't say whether Leah was involved in the decision to trick Jacob and marry him, but after they got married, he exclaimed to his father-in-law, "What is this you have done to me?" (Genesis 29:25). After their weeklong honeymoon, Jacob married Rachael, the sister he really loved.

Then came an all-too-familiar occurrence—although her husband didn't really love her, Leah started having children. She hoped her children would make Jacob love her. She named her first son Reuben, meaning "See, a son!" When Reuben didn't make Jacob love her, she named her second son Simeon, meaning "heard." She named her third son Levi, which means "attached." She thought that after three sons perhaps her husband would be attached to her, but that didn't turn out to be the case.

"Where's my future husband?" This question, asked by multitudes of single women suggests that it's in God's plan for them to be married and it should be in their time, not God's time. But have they considered that the Lord might be protecting them from the wrong people seeking to enter their lives only to lure them away from Him? Have they considered that trying to "make" others love them isn't the way to go?

Their hearts are in the right place, but society tells them they should be elsewhere. Their hearts tell them to dress modestly, but society tells them to dress up like ladies of the night. Their hearts tell them to wait until God speaks, but society tells them to catch mates while they can. Their hearts tell them the apple is forbidden, but society tells them to eat it and become like God (Genesis 3:5).

Flesh-worshipping thoughts like these are common; thoughts that glorify God are rare. The lessons of history are clear: You will not change him. You cannot remake him. You cannot do anything to change thus says the Lord—"Wait, I say!"

An awesome place to be!

> Being single, despite what (literally) most of the world
> says, is not inferior to being married. It's an opportunity
> for us to develop a love story with God.[35]

First off, whose big idea is it that you have to pair up or hook up? So
what if your biological clock is ticking? Did no one tell you it's better
to be alone than be hooked up and miserable? Did no one tell you can't
hurry love although you can hurry lust? And this obsession about babies,
and showers, and Facebook pictures, and whose kid is cuter than whose.
Get real! This is a real world with real responsibilities and real situations,
so don't underestimate the importance of waiting before you commit to
a lifelong responsibility.

Your body belongs to God, and you are its caretaker, so you owe not
one bit of yourself to anyone else until you're wedded. For this reason,
you don't need to feel awkward or guilty about saying no! There are so
many fishes in the sea, and it behooves you to wait until the tide rises
and the right fish are biting before you make a move. And when you're
"hooked" up with God, He will decide both the fishing site and the fish
to hook you up with. Meanwhile, "Live in the sunshine, swim the sea,
drink the wild air," said Ralph Waldo Emerson. Your womanhood is
not defined by society's prescription.

> A woman is not born a woman. Nor does she become
> one when she marries a man, bears a child and does
> their dirty linen, not even when she joins a woman's
> liberation movement. A woman becomes a woman
> when she becomes what God wants her to be.[36]

God is saying to the single woman, "I dare you to trust me to lead you
to that right husband … I dare you to pray the heavens open and watch

---

35 Guardians of Purity, p. 164, Julie Hiramine, Published 2012, Charisma House.

36 Jackie Kendall & Debby Jones "Lady in Waiting: Becoming God's Best While
    Waiting for Mr. Right); Destiny Image Publishers.

me—I, God, turn the glory on." So if you are single at this very moment, thank God and consider yourself blessed for the opportunity to become thoroughly immersed in His work! "Wait for the LORD; be strong and take heart and wait for the LORD" (Psalm 27:14 NIV).

The Lesson of Abraham and Sarah

When God told Abraham and Sarah that Sarah would conceive, they laughed at what under other circumstances would have been an insult. Sarah, who was ninety, had long since given up on the idea she would ever bear children by her husband, who was also quite old. There's no clear evidence that Sarah fell prostrate before God and communed with Him for His will to be done in her life. There is evidence, however, that she had thrown in the towel. She no longer believed that through God all things were possible, and she concluded that God needed their help. She gave Hagar to Abram as a concubine.

Although strange to us today, Sarah's plan was quite ingenious. According to ancient customs, a female slave could legally serve as a surrogate mother for her barren mistress, so Sarah could count any child born from her husband and Hagar as her own. The plan produce a child but not the child God had promised. This is what happens when we choose our will instead of God's will for our lives.

> In this story we have a powerful example of how when faced with daunting circumstances, even a great man of God had a lapse of faith. In Genesis 17:18, 19, Abraham pleaded with God to accept Ishmael as his heir; the Lord, of course, rejected that offer. The only "miraculous" element in the birth of Ishmael was Sarah's willingness to share her husband with another woman! There was nothing out of the ordinary about the birth of a child to this woman, a child born "according to the flesh." Had Abraham trusted in what God had promised him instead of letting the circumstances overcome that trust,

none of this would have happened, and a lot of grief would have been avoided.[37]

The dishonor Abraham and Sarah brought on themselves, their families, their community, and more important on God serves as a warning to the rest of humankind: we must wait on God without conditions! A good test of our unwavering faith in Him is whether His commands govern our lives exclusively or if we put our own conditions on Him. We must always rest on the principle that God is faithful God who will keep His covenant of love as He has done in times past.

> Know therefore that the LORD your God is God; he is the faithful God, keeping his covenant of love to a thousand generations of those who love him and keep his commands. (Deuteronomy 7:9)

Trust God's Timing

"For I know the plans I have for you, declares the LORD, plans to prosper you and not to harm you, plans to give you hope and a future" (Jeremiah 29:11).

"O Lord, you know my inward thoughts. From the foundations of the earth, you have considered my future. When I am near you, my nearness is felt; when my thoughts wander far away, you are there to bring me into alignment with your will. Purge my thoughts and cause them to be consistently focused on only you. O Lord, you have established time and order. You know when to open doors and when to shut them; you understand my needs, and you can adjust my chemistry. You've said that no good thing will you withhold from your children. I trust you now to send me a helpmate fit for your queen. But first, make me ready to accept that which you are getting ready to grant. I claim your promises, and I rest upon your word."

---

37 SDA Bible Commentary, November 2011.

If we are ever to be happy the way God wants us to be, we have to become vulnerable and allow God to lead us through the twists and turns of life, over the potholes and out of the trenches; we have to trust Him implicitly. We must never fall into the Enemy's trap of impatience, for when we do, we become desperate and rush through doors God intended to be closed. Too often we get carried away with the thrill of the moment in new relationships and conveniently ignore the red flags. When this happens, it's impossible to identify the qualities and characteristics necessary for a healthy, long-term relationship; the result is always a disappointing experience.

Someone asked what God's posture is when we decide to make things happen on our own. Will He still love us, or will He sit idly by and allow us to suffer? God's love is always unconditional, but if we push hard enough and long enough to have things our way, God will sometimes allow us to veer off His planned path for us and often to our detriment. Why go against godly counsel? If He sets you up, it's never to have you fail; it's for your good and His glory.

Don't listen to those voices coming from your biological clock; consider the bright side of waiting on God. When you've prayed and prayed some more, after you've been battered, bruised, and knocked down because you've been obediently waiting, God will usher you out of your dark days and will bring you into the light of His glory and grace. There is only one voice that's worth listening to: "Wait for the LORD; be strong and take heart and wait for the LORD" (Psalm 27:14).

Chapter Ten

ENJOY YOUR FINAL DESCENT

No man (woman) who is worth a dime will talk
disparagingly about a former partner.

I was on a flight to the beautiful island of Barbados for a Christian women's meeting. A few minutes into the flight, after that "You may walk about …" announcement, a stunning woman next to me (she could have been in her early seventies with a classy up-do and a distinct British accent) asked me out of the blue if I was married. She had noticed I wasn't wearing a ring. You know the drill—the humming sound in the aircraft makes talking comfortable, you see people in conversation but can't hear them. I was relaxed, engaging in our conversation.

"You're correct," I replied. "I'm unmarried." The lady smiled admiringly before she said, "But not for long perhaps?" I gave off hearty laughter. The cocktail cart interrupted our conversation, which gave me time to observe my friend's stunning diamond on her ring finger. We received our apple juice, easy ice, and adjusted ourselves to accommodate the trays. The interruption was welcome as it gave me time to collect my thoughts.

"Your first time to Barbados?" Coleen asked.

"Actually, my second."

"What's taking you there?"

After I revealed that I was participating in women's Christian conference, Coleen confirmed she was also.

We talked about how God believes in singleness at any age, some of the issues facing singles, and about the joys of singleness. We agreed that finding a good Christian companion in later years can be challenging. Coleen raised her rock to show me; she was turning seventy, she was engaged, and she was living life at its best. She had met her fiancé on a flight to Australia a year earlier. She admitted that during her ten years of singleness she never once was preoccupied with remarriage. Her work for the Lord, she said, kept her fulfilled, and the story of Sarah and the fact that God makes good on His promises was always on her front burner.

I took away from my encounter with Sarah several things not dependent on pop culture or any social determinants but truisms rooted in the incontrovertible promises of God.

> » "Delight yourself in the LORD, and he will give you the desires of your heart. Commit your way to the LORD; trust in him, and he will act" (Psalm 37:4–5) and "My God will meet all your needs according to the riches of his glory in Christ Jesus" (Philippians 4:19).

> » When we delight ourselves in the Lord, we become so busy with the things of God that our minds, hearts, and souls are immersed in His work. We focus on kingdom building and helping others grow and serve, so we aren't obsessed with looking for love in all the wrong places; we focus on the greatest love of all, Jesus Christ, who promised to supply all our needs.

» "The Lord is not slow in keeping his promise, as some understand slowness. Instead he is patient with you, not wanting anyone to perish, but everyone to come to repentance" (2 Peter 3:9).

» Coleen was patient. She had not become obsessed with mate-hunting but had immersed herself in the work of the Lord, became great at her craft, and celebrated her singleness. That was when she met the man of her dreams!

But the reverse of Coleen's experience is what happens when we become impatient with God: nothing moves, time stands still, doubts pile up. This is dangerous and dicey.

In another chapter, we witnessed the pickle Sarah got her family into when she refused to wait on the fulfillment of God's promise and chose to entice her husband to bed with the maid. What do you think happens when we run after the promised one when God has His ram in the thicket? Brows furrow. Palms sweat. Nerves go to war. We want what we want now! Children know when the sun is setting that it's time to end the fun. We too know when we are out of God's will, but we continue to play well after sunset. Wouldn't it be a good idea to read Sarah's bio?

"When we fail to wait prayerfully for God's guidance and strength, we are saying with our actions if not our lips, that we do not need him" says Charles Hummel.

When I really began to believe in God, somewhere in my late teens, I began to put certain pieces of my earlier childhood together, and though a few pieces of the puzzle were missing here and there, the outline began to take shape. The more I looked at my life's puzzle, the more I realized that it must have been God who healed me after the family horse Tony ran over me, that He brought me back to consciousness after I fell out of a coconut tree, and that God's grace and mercy had revived me after the doctors turned the lights out in my hospital room. You are even more important to God at this stage of your life because you are more available to do His work. So all those things you thought impossible because of family constraints, do them!

I hope you have done some planning for your retirement years and will enjoy them. If by chance you become dependent to any extent on your children, don't feel guilty about that after all you've done for them and the investments you made in their future at the expense of personal gratification. Consider it payback time!

Regardless of what pop culture portrays, what an awesome opportunity you have! Behold the God of second chances who makes all things new. Remain pure—don't dwell on the flesh stuff, and most definitely don't allow desperation for the flesh and old regrets to rush you between the sheets.

Look at things this way: You are free from the misery, shame, resentment, and emotional roller coaster of turbulent relationships, so don't revisit them. Looking back is never productive; keep your eyes focused on new and bright things as you make your final descent. You're in charge now, and if you've never been propped up like a queen before, now is your chance. You have a double blessing—you are a child of the Most High, and you have a right to live that way! No longer will you auction off your innocence only to feel secondhand or valueless feelings that botched sexual relationships bring. What if you never get another chance to cuddle between the sheets? Then cuddle alone. Claim the promises of God. Be true to yourself. Be true to your faith. Trust God's promises.

Because you're aging doesn't mean sexual sins won't tempt you. There still will be hungry, confused vultures in waiting. To quote Princess Elizabeth of Yugoslavia, "A man needs the sexual conquest to prove he can still do it … It's like having a duel with himself. He has to prove it all the time. We [women] don't have to prove it."

How Old Is Too Old?

Each stage of life has its downsides, but each also has its thrills. Which stage is the most enjoyable is an unfair question in that it's open for widely differing interpretations, but years of wisdom, experience, and often wealth is the perfect setup for your final descent. So what's your hesitation? It's true that Father Time can wreak havoc on the body, a lack of hormones may have diminished some urges, but the peace and contentment that came from a life lived in service of God more than match an appealing "Hollywood" body.

If you are prone to wallow in pity, think again—your life has been disrupted but only to a point and in a specific sense; never let anyone condemn or thwart your reversal of fortune. There are seasons of life, and this is yours, so find joy in it.

Wherever your final descent finds you, don't settle for anything less than God's best. You've served others with distinction and you've honored God's Word; now it is time to put Him to the test. He wants to take your hand and lead you through your final descent. Enjoy the walk! "Being confident of this, that he who began a good work in you will carry it on to completion until the day of Christ Jesus" (Philippians 1:6).

Personal Inventory for the Single Person

Check "yes" if you agree, "no" if you don't.

I am single and loving it.   ☐ yes   ☐ no

I am often lonely and depressed.   ☐ yes   ☐ no

I am praying for a mate.   ☐ yes   ☐ no

I am praying for God's mate.   ☐ yes   ☐ no

I spend most of my spare time in ministry.   ☐ yes   ☐ no

I am not involved in ministry.   ☐ yes   ☐ no

I spend most of my time watching television.   ☐ yes   ☐ no

I spend most of my time on Facebook.   ☐ yes   ☐ no

I spend most of my time texting or talking on the phone. ☐ yes ☐ no

I spend most of my time at the mall. ☐ yes ☐ no

I am enjoying good health. ☐ yes ☐ no

My health is challenging. ☐ yes ☐ no

I have wonderful friends. ☐ yes ☐ no

I have a supportive family. ☐ yes ☐ no

I am living my best life yet. ☐ yes ☐ no

Chapter Eleven

BLEMISHED SHEETS AND GOD'S GRACE

My grace is sufficient for you, for my power is made perfect in weakness.
—2 CORINTHIANS 12:9

Have you ever gone back far enough to figure out when you started enjoying forbidden fruit and why? When due to your disbelief that God would provide, you ran ahead of God and fantasized with someone who should have been off limits? The Lord is inviting you to come to Him to settle the matter. "Though your sins are like scarlet, they shall be as white as snow; though they are red as crimson, they shall be like wool" (Isaiah 1:18).

Recalling past experiences can be beneficial as long as such memories don't discourage you but lead you to the cross. When God in His mercy takes us wicked and stubborn people and massages us with His balm of mercy and grace, He counts us as clean. What a wonderful Savior who Himself has been touched with our infirmities! God's pardoning, infinite, and unrestricted grace is an amazing gift available to all. It comes at the most pivotal point of our greatest needs. Why should we allow ourselves to be lost by neglecting so great a grace? Measureless grace is what we could expect to receive when we take God at His word—the assurance that He forgives and forgets. How far and how long will He continue to pardon? Into the depths of the sea, and He will remember them no more! Why are you reluctant to surrender your blemished sheets when all you have to do is yield to God's tugging on your heart?

Helen, a high school sophomore, had fallen far behind in school and was facing the possibility of failing tenth grade. Having learned this in a parent-teacher meeting, the mother calmly told the math teacher, "In our house, failure is not an option, so this morning I'm asking you for patience and God for grace." The more the teacher tried to convince Helen's mother that there was no hope for her child, the more the mother stuck to her guns. As the semester progressed, Helen, a D-minus student, began after-school tutoring sessions. Weeks passed. The midterm report came out. The nightmare was over. That D minus had become a B plus!

That's what happens when we believe in the power of God to turn things around—a blemished record of failure can turn into a spotless record of triumph. But here is where we need to make special note: there is no magic way to earn higher grades, and there is mystery in how God can make filthy wrinkled sheets as white as snow. However, to nip discouragement in the bud, we need to know God is in the business of pardoning even the vilest sinner, but we must also know that to avoid a lifetime of heartaches, we must follow God's principles in scripture. We must learn life's crucial lessons well because time is not always on our side.

So much more could be said about the wisdom in timely obedience and the fact that God credits us for our diligence. So many times we lose out simply because we have been taught that because God is loving and kind, He will forgive our failings no matter what we've done or for how long we've been rebelling. However, that thinking is only partially true; the real truth is that the penalty for some transgressions is irreversible, meaning it can never be recalled, and while God will indeed forgive, we must pay a certain price for our waywardness.

The Heart of the Matter

Work with me as I develop and analogy between a gift you are required to keep unopened until your birthday and the innocence God wants you to save for your marriage day. You can feel where I'm going with this. I dare you to open your gift before your birthday and still experience the same degree of ecstasy that you would have had on "the" anticipated day if you had left it wrapped up! I double dare you to deny that saving your jewels for marriage would have yielded more joy, trust, and respect in your relationship than you had to settle for because you chose the promiscuous path of picking fruit before harvest time. Once we settle that our decision was ill-advised and was not in concert with God's plan, we can recalculate our journey. That's why we have a Savior—that's why we have a Lord touched with our infirmity yet without sin. He knows our frailties and weaknesses; He longs to cover our nakedness, work with us through our blotches, and remake us into His pure vessels as if we had never violated our values.

What do you do when Jesus has put you on notice that He is getting ready to cleanse your sheets and turn things around? You know in your heart of hearts that letting go is hard. You think about getting through the lonely nights. You think about the shift that's coming and whether you can stand the cold. The rent's due and you wonder if you can pay it on your own. You know it's going to be rough. The day will take longer to break, and the birds will begin their chants just a little later; even their songs will be less upbeat.

But morning must break, and your wobbly knees must bend to the Creator who has promised to tame the flesh that more than before (now that you're in the heat of the battle) will be turned up a hundred times hotter. But along comes Galatians 5:17, which gives a picture of this controversy between flesh and spirit: "For the flesh desires what is contrary to the Spirit and the Spirit what is contrary to the flesh. They are in conflict with each other, so that you are not to do whatever you want."

Flesh and spirit—what a war. Paul reminds us that left to our own devices, we will not bring our flesh under the authority of God. But when we resolve to adopt a new way of living, God applies His grace and gives us victory over the flesh and the enemy. Here is the conclusion of the controversy between the two rivals—spirit and flesh—in Galatians 2:20: "I have been crucified with Christ and I no longer live, but Christ lives in me. The life I now live in the body, I live by faith in the Son of God, who loved me and gave himself for me."

Today, throngs of women of all ages have not been able to wrap their heads around Galatians 2:20; they find themselves in a dark place and unable to relinquish relationships they know are not in accordance with God's will. How to navigate their way from blemished sheets to a better place is often a big challenge, but they should know there is no place so dark that God's escape route cannot illuminate a path from it.

But even when this point has been settled, there is the hurdle of the flesh that is so often irrational to contend with—to be pressured to hop between forbidden sheets or to be branded a failure by letting him go! The child of God will possibly look to the life of Joseph to find courage to do the right thing; for even lifelong Christians are thrown for a loop when they face quandaries of the flesh.

Joseph found himself in a moral dilemma when he had to decide between nuzzling in prohibited sheets with Potiphar's wife or pleasing God who had made it abundantly clear we should flee fornication and not commit adultery. The record does not suggest any other motive for Joseph's refusal to sleep with his master's wife other than to do so would be to have sinned against God.

But the story does not end there; the writer of Genesis records the price Joseph paid for his faithfulness to God.

> When his master heard the story his wife told him,
> saying, this is how your slave treated me, he burned with
> anger. Joseph's master took him and put him in prison,
> the place where the king's prisoners were confined.
> (Genesis 3:19–20)

Like Joseph, we can expect to be maligned or worse when we snub worldly norms in favor of sexual purity. Joseph's story could be your story, because God now, as in times of old, always has a handsome reward at the end of every test. Joseph became ruler of Egypt, and those who may have found humor in his refusal to bed with the diva had an opportunity to reevaluate their opinion—it was not cowardice after all but exercised and unrestrained Christ in Joseph.

Joseph chose not to "enjoy the pleasures of sin for a season," to get caught up in blemished sheets. He knew he could not offer his master total devotion while being inappropriate with his wife. So how much is God's grace worth? How much are you prepared to give up for your allegiance to Him? When the time comes that you're faced with "leaving the coat behind" or escaping the clutches of immorality, ask, "Lord, what would you have me to do?" In those moments, lean on God—believe that His grace is sufficient.

From the Prison to the Palace—Grace All the Way

Had Joseph become bitter with God after having been a faithful follower but suffering in prison, he would not have learned the awesome lessons he did. Joseph was like Job, another faithful follower of God who found grace in God's eyes. He was determined to endure the backlash for a crime he had not committed; he knew the God he served would supply the grace he needed in times of discouragement and would deliver him.

> But while Joseph was there in the prison, the Lord was
> with him; he showed him kindness and granted him
> favor in the eyes of the prison warden. So the warden

put Joseph in charge of all those held in the prison, and
he was made responsible for all that was done there. The
warden paid no attention to anything under Joseph's
care, because the Lord was with Joseph and gave him
success in whatever he did. (Genesis 39:21–23)

Another Snapshot of Grace

She was only twenty-nine and already a grandmother. At first, I couldn't
believe what was in front of me until I rechecked the parent contact
card. Actually, she looked twenty-nine from her facial appearance, but
her beautiful, smooth, tan skin plastered with tattoos of guys' names
that snaked across her almost bare chest until they vanished between
her breasts made it tough to tell.

I looked at the daughter she had come to collect early from a class she
was already failing. You don't normally press parents for a reason when
they tell you they're picking up a child early for personal reasons, but
I threw caution to the wind and asked. I got an answer I didn't want
to hear: "She needs to be with her child because I have to work." She
worked as a stripper at some bare-bottom club. Almost as a gesture of
rebellion, the grandmother handed me a pass to watch her show the
following evening. I said thanks, that I would think about it. I gave her
a card with the name of my church and my cell number. She took it,
read it, and left with her daughter.

I continued to teach; it was Wednesday. The day's lesson was to be about
hyperboles and onomatopoeias, but not much got done, I'm embarrassed
to admit—my mind was otherwise occupied. When the bell rang, I was
relieved. I headed home more relaxed, but what was on my mind was
the stripper grandmother—that's how I remembered her, the lady who
corrupted her offspring with her selfish antics.

When we hear testimonies about God's grace and blemished sheets, we
often think about Bible characters such as Bathsheba and Rahab and

the Samaritan woman, but this Mary was my point of grace, and you'll understand why.

When I got home, I read my e-mails. Need I tell you the first one was from Mary? She asked to join me for worship that week. The days leading up to worship service were filled with anticipation: who would show up, Mary the tattooed stripper or Mary something else?

I was in church, dressed in my church suit, hair neatly coiffured. The praise team was about to step on the rostrum. A lady entered my pew, and I politely moved over to make room. I nodded at her, and she smiled. "This is Mary," she said innocently. "I told you I'd come." Mary and I broke down in tears. She was dressed to worship—tailored suit and covered tattoos. I could fill in the details, but suffice it to say Mary never stopped worshipping. This all took place in 2004, and she's a committed follower of Christ to this day.

Meet Mary again, the rogue mother who almost drowned in despair, in a quicksand in which each club gig provided stimulus for the next. Mary could see no way out of her circumstances and had thrown in the towel on purity, but morning broke, the fog cleared. Just when the Enemy was putting his party together, the rain of God's mercy fell—not a sprinkle but a deluge. What a pivotal grace and mercy moment it was when Christ showed up. When He did, Mary's bio of blemished sheets and carnal desires was forever updated—that's because demons flee from between sordid sheets when Jesus shows up!

Oh how the depth of God's grace amazes me! Every day, He rescues men and women from strip clubs and bars. These souls are God's diamonds in the rough waiting to be loved back into His fold. Mary the stripper—what a story of God's mercy and grace. Mary the misguided parent was snatched from the stronghold of the Enemy for eternity. "And she went into the town and told the men: 'Come; see a man who told me everything I ever did. Could this be the Messiah?'" (John 4:29).

Chapter Twelve

FORGIVEN

To forgive is to set a prisoner free and discover that the prisoner was you.
—LEWIS B. SMEDES

*Man has two great spiritual needs. One is for
forgiveness. The other is for goodness.*
—BILLY GRAHAM

*Forgiveness is the fragrance that the violet
sheds on the heel that has crushed it.*
—MARK TWAIN

*Forgiveness is like an etch a sketch ... You make an error, shake the
etch a sketch and the error is erased instantly. Likewise with God,
we sin; God wipes the slate clean and gives us a new outlook.*
—DOREEN PRISCILLA BROWN

The Struggles of Forgiving

I was hanging on for dear life, struggling with tremendous guilt after a divorce. Someone once said that the "arm of flesh will fail you," and I wondered if I was living out that expression. I had never been surrounded by so many people and yet I had never felt so alone. People have a way of conveniently forgetting their own gorges in life and deliberately try to weigh you down with guilt trips of the "what ifs" and "I told you so." Today, I advise folks struggling emotionally and reliving their pasts to move on with or without the blessings of others who can't or don't desire to recognize their plights. I warn them that not every card they receive is worth its postage stamp, that not every e-mail comes from an empathetic source.

You have to own your own hurt and determine in your heart that with Jesus, you can make it in spite of your circumstances. This is common sense, but it is also scriptural. God doesn't sit on a pedestal watching you steam in regret and anger. His plan is not to give sinners black eyes and send them away without vision but to heal them and restore them to a right relationship with Him. "I am come that they might have life and have it more abundantly" (John 10:10).

Gosh—it took me a long time to get it! Someone reminded me that it's more difficult to forgive yourself when your offense is willful, meaning that when you knew better. But whether it's willful or unintentional, refusal to forgive yourself is a detrimental decision that signals something far more disturbing deep inside—it's an inclination to relish pride, which disappoints God; it indicates to Him that despite your declaration of trust in Him, you still have a spirit of pride and stubbornness rather than the freedom He provides; consider it an enema that would allow you to move on without spiritual constipation and end up with God in His kingdom.

The two imageries here are in stark opposition to God's plans to have us living without spiritual constipation: pride and stubbornness, and freedom, a spiritual enema. You cannot remain paralyzed by the guilt of your past when you have purposed to ascend to the new heights to which God has called you. Even today, God knows you'd be struggling with the challenge of forgiveness, so He said, "Truly I tell you, unless you change and become like little children, you will never enter the kingdom of heaven" (Matthew 18:3).

Barriers to Forgiveness

If sin has been confessed, repented of, and forgiven, it's time to move on. Remember, "If anyone is in Christ, he is a new creation; the old has gone, the new has come!" (2 Corinthians 5:17). Part of the "old" that has gone is the remembrance of past sins and the guilt they produced. Sadly, some Christians are prone to wallowing in memories of their former sinful lives, memories that should have been dead and buried long ago. This is pointless; it runs counter to the victorious Christian life God wants for us. An anonymous person once said, "If God has saved you out of a sewer, don't dive back in and swim around."

Too often we get in our own way through our refusal to forgive ourselves; we fly in the face of God when we swim around in pride and self-pity. What did Christ do with our sins on Calvary? Were they not nailed to the cross with Him? Is it fair then to stew in self-pity as if we were still in bondage? We cannot believe Satan's lie if we are to live in victory. "Whom the Son sets free, is free indeed" (John 8:36). Jeremiah 31:34 offers us a poignant insight into the pattern God has set for us to follow. "He remembers our sins no more." Isaiah 43:25 says, "I, even I, am the one who wipes out your transgressions for my own sake; and I will not remember your sins." Remembering our sins—not dwelling on them—should serve one purpose only: to remind us of the magnitude of God's forgiveness. This will makes it easier for us to forgive others.

Other Barriers

What happens when we refuse to admit our faults? How can we possibly move on unless we admit our wrongdoing? Some people claim to have moved on even though there has been no admission of wrong. Think about it—forgiveness is not only for the person who has been injured but also for the person who committed the injury. There's something miraculous that happens when fault is acknowledged; the moment is magical. But pride will say, "Don't forgive, because it makes you look weak." Broken fellowship with God and with our neighbor—what a pickle! God says, "You cannot have fellowship with me if you fail to forgive. Lewis B. Smedes says, "To forgive is to set a prisoner free and discover that the prisoner was you."

Denial, Accepting Forgiveness, and Confession

At one meeting of women in my Divorce Recovery sessions in our church fellowship hall, Paulette, in her early fifties, was still grappling with the issues of forgiveness well after her divorce two decades earlier. Here was a woman who had made serving in her church a staple. When she wasn't leading song service, she was playing the piano or expressively raising "holy hands" in response to the worship service. All the while, the effects of her inability to humble herself before God and put an end to the stronghold of holding grudges was becoming more obvious. Eventually, her health began to fail (at least she thought it was), and it seemed every week she had a testimony about some ailment she was treated for but none of which could be diagnosed.

It's your turn to look in the mirror to see whether you too are engaging in physical bluffs and mind games because of your failure to forgive. The fact is that only you are concerned with the details of your marital indiscretions, Christ isn't! He wants you to throw yourself a forgiveness party and invite David, a man after His own heart, as a special guest. What a toast David would give! "Then I acknowledged my sin to you and did not cover up my iniquity. I said, 'I will confess my transgressions to the LORD'" (Psalm 32).

Realizing that our sins are forgiven should make it easier to forgive others their sins (Matthew 7:1–5; 1 Timothy 1:15). Forgiveness should remind us of the great Savior who forgave us, undeserving though we will always be, and draw us closer in loving obedience to Him (Romans 5:10; Psalm 103:2–3,10–14). Whenever our sins come to our thoughts, we must never wallow in them with regrets; the fact that God has already forgiven us gives clearance to move on to the next chapter in our lives.

But watch how Satan works: he will use our past against us and make us believe we are wretched, not good enough to move on to anything. That's when we need to remain strong and remember that God is a God of mercy and grace and that He saves to the utmost *all* who come to Him in true repentance. How vile a sinner must you be before God will dismiss you? The answer to this question is the good news already expressed in Isaiah 43:25: "I, even I, am he who blots out your transgressions, for my own sake, and remembers your sins no more."

Do I Really Believe?

At the heart of not forgiving oneself is the trap of unbelief and faithlessness that's accompanied by joylessness. The burden of not knowing that God has forgiven our shameful acts will not allow us to release ourselves from the past and move forward to bigger and better things. What a burden! Failure to forgive ourselves will rob us of the liberty Christ granted us on the cross. Forgiveness is the great liberator that frees us from the past. Forgiveness banishes guilt and shame and enables us to bask in the glow of Christ's sacrifice for us.

Consider these scriptures as part of the forgiveness process.

> » 2 Corinthians 5:17: "Therefore if any man be in Christ, he is a new creature: old things are passed away; behold all things are become new."

> » Hebrews 9:14: "How much more shall the blood of Christ, who through the eternal Spirit offered himself without spot to God, purge your conscience from dead works to serve the living God?"

> » 2 Peter 1:9: "But he that lacketh these things is blind, and cannot see afar off, and hath forgotten that he was purged from his old sins."

> » Colossians 3:13: "Forbearing one another, and forgiving one another, if any man have a quarrel against any: even as Christ forgave you, so also do ye."

> » Hebrews 12:15: "Looking diligently lest any man fail of the grace of God; lest any root of bitterness springing up trouble you, and thereby many be defiled."

> » Hebrews 4:16: "Let us therefore come boldly unto the throne of grace that we may obtain mercy, and find grace to help in time of need."

If you ever become conflicted about your ability to forgive yourself and others, if you feel powerless and insignificant, as if your role in the act of forgiveness may not matter, recognize that it matters every bit and that more important, the price for your redemption has been paid. It's up to you understand that the blood of Jesus Christ, so powerful, so potent, wipes the slate clean and treats your past as if you had never sinned. Don't make the mistake of so many others by thinking forgiveness requires some effort on your part. Apart from yielding to the Holy Spirit and relying completely on God to gift you with the ability to forgive, all you need is a willing heart; God will take care of the rest.

Ponder this.

> The experience of forgiveness ends the sinner's vulnerability to God's wrath and clears away any barriers to reconciliation and fellowship between God and humans. A new life opens up for the sinner, who has the privilege of living in fellowship with Christ under the direction and guidance of the Holy Spirit.[38]

If you say your moral life has not been perfect, welcome to the community of flawed people! Even if you have violated your sheet standards, God's grace is sufficient to clean you up and help you move on. God's grand and noble grace is not performance-based or dependent on the extent of your failings. Today, may you find the strength and the peace of a loving Father through both the reality and the experience of His forgiveness, and "May the God of hope fill you with all joy and peace

---

38 General Conference of SDA Adult Sabbath School Bible Study Guide book, 35.

in believing, so that by the power of the Holy Spirit you may abound in hope" (Romans 15:13).

Now that God through Christ has forgiven your indiscretions, you must release yourself from that dark place of self-mutilation and forgive yourself.

> Finally, brothers and sisters, whatever is true, whatever is noble, whatever is right, whatever is pure, whatever is lovely, whatever is admirable—if anything is excellent or praiseworthy—think about such things. (Philippians 4:8)

Chapter Thirteen

RESTITUTION AND RESTORATION

Throughout history no one has suffered more than God. He has suffered because his own children fell away from him. Ever since the Fall, God has been working tirelessly for the restoration of mankind. People do not know this brokenhearted aspect of God.
—SUN MYUNG MOON

"Come now, let us settle the matter," says the Lord. Though your sins are like scarlet, they shall be as white as snow; though they are red as crimson, they shall be like wool."
—ISAIAH 1:18–20

Scandalous Grace

*I*t's hard to relight a fire after you've let it die, but in no way do you want to second-guess Christ's power to turn ashes into beauty. You won't second-guess him, but you have to marvel at what Christ had in mind when He extended this invitation. After the sheets have been dirtied by shame, why would Christ seem so anxious to wash them white as snow? Why would He be so adamant about restoring sinners unto himself? Does He not remember what God said in Jeremiah 17:9,

"The heart is deceitful above all things and beyond cure"? But knowing how hopeless we would be without help, God sent His blameless, sinless Son to redeem us from the curse of sin.

This act of Christ taking our place has astounded so many in our time, but He clearly described the highest act of love imaginable, the greatest sacrifice the world has ever witnessed: "For God so loved the world that he gave his one and only Son, that whoever believes in him shall not perish but have eternal life" (John 3:16).

Life Happens

God knows our hearts and that in the course of our struggles with our sinful nature we would make a mess of things. In those moments when we are ashamed, when we look at our lives and our conduct is nothing more than a slap in the face of a generous God, when we wrestle like Paul, knowing the good that we should but follow flesh instead, God wants us to consider John 3:16 with particular emphasis on "whoever." It makes no difference that the struggles may have been abhorrent sheet things that should have been reserved until Jesus could be present, but now we are left with social and spiritual baggage!

Are you ready for the good news? God, who knew you from the beginning, has been expecting this moment! "Come now," He says. You think you've made such a horrific mess of your life by your sexual sins and bouncing from one illicit relationship to the other. You think there's nothing you can do to get back in the good graces of God, but Christ says you're not a write-off. That's what the Enemy would make you believe; but don't believe it. Embrace the grace God has extended you and prepare for a makeover!

Nothing is ever wasted with God, a specialist in restoring shards to wholeness. Though God is displeased with the sin, He could never be more in love with the sinner. Because of the magnitude of our sin, we may be tempted to believe we are too wicked for God to forgive; but the Bible teaches that God desires all of us to be saved. The examples of David, Solomon, and the woman at the well among so many others illustrate God's willingness to forgive even the most errant sinners. Just as God has forgiven those who have messed up, He will also graciously accept your contrition if you willingly surrender all to Him.

That He forgives and restores so generously is no fallacy—that's just God's nature! He knows our sin-driven hearts; no matter how much we have fallen short, Jesus' death provides us an escape. It's never too late to turn around. And what an intimidating thought it is to be offered an escape to atone for our vile deficiencies! It almost suggests that we could expect to get a bill in the mail. But there is no expectation for payment except that we surrender all and accept Christ's invitation to newness in Him.

So what do we do? We release the guilt. We surrender the shame. We renounce our fears. We cease the self-condemnation, everything that tells us we're too wretched to deserve second chances. Not only will God rescue us from our predicament, He will also dip us in the storehouse of His grace and give us enough to cover our past. Though the consequences of our mistakes and bad choices may remain, because God is faithful and loves us so much, He will impute even more grace to aid us; His door of mercy is open wide. Let David's experiences with sexual failings and the peace he eventually found in God's love and mercy take on new meaning in our lives.

> Be merciful to me, O God; because of your great mercy wipe away my sins! I recognize my faults; I am always conscious of my sins … Remove my sin and I will be clean; wash me, and I will be whiter than snow … Create a pure heart in me, O God, and put a new and loyal spirit in me … Give me again the joy that comes from your salvation, and make me willing to obey you … Spare my life, O God, and save me, and I will gladly proclaim your righteousness. (Psalm 51:1–14)[39]

---

39 Happiness Digest, 10, Discovering the secret of endless joy.

I was speaking at a Women's Day worship service on "The Brook Is Dry." The kernel of the message was what we should do when we reach dead ends in life. In the middle of the altar call, a middle-aged woman hurried down the aisle sobbing. She was remorseful and desperate. The consequences of her past sexual escapades had been catching up with her. The tears were flowing, and the stress was building. Life was spinning in real time. Her testimony was far from self-effacing; she was terribly ashamed of the poor sexual choices she had made and was reaching out for support. When the voice of Jesus calls, you don't worry about looking dignified—you just answer!

I recall the moment I came to faith in Christ. At first, I was shell-shocked, worried that people would think such and such and draw false conclusions. They possibly did, but that's never important. That lady understood this, and her actions that morning changed her life. Laboring for the cause of Christ is all about experiencing the move of God in the hearts of those without hope. This is the moment those who labor in the vineyard work for.

Oh what a relief it is when we cease fighting against our own will and submit to God's. There's nothing better!

> The warfare against self is the greatest battle that was ever fought. The yielding of self, surrendering all to the will of God, requires a struggle; but the soul must submit to God before it can be renewed in holiness."[40]

Kissed by God

If our society is to return to its spiritual roots in which God is viewed as the alpha and the omega and not just a "go to" source in times of crisis, it will take a mighty move of the Holy Spirit to accomplish this through the testimonies of broken and contrite hearts. How will God speak? Through a financial crisis? Famine? Pestilence? War? Who will

---

40 *Steps to Christ*, 42.

speak to the people on behalf of God? God will choose! But here is the good news, a poignant promise that God seeks not to ever leave His children defenseless. In 2 Chronicles 7:14, we are provided with this sobering text.

> If my people, who are called by my name, will humble themselves and pray and seek my face and turn from their wicked ways, then I will hear from heaven, and I will forgive their sin and will heal their land.

Cynics will be suspicious, and stiff-necked people will resist, but God will remain relentless in His quest to save us.

> Our Savior is trying all the time to draw people's minds away from worldly pleasures to the wonderful blessings that Christ can give. To these people who are trying to find water in the dry wells of the world, He (Jesus) says, "Come, whoever is thirsty, accept the water of life as a gift, whoever wants it."[41]

This is such a poignant reminder that even when we don't get it all right, though we may have sunken to debasing depths, God is such a forgiving God and is willing and ready to sanitize the impurities from between the sheets and make all things new. He is the God of second chances!

When the debates end, all the highbrow nuances will boil down to one simple truth: because we live in a fallen world, we have been subjected to some degree of moral turpitude. David's story of a sexually depraved man with no moral compass and drunk with lust and power but still so favored by our Father offers a much profounder lesson—that though God will hold us accountable for our wrongs, He so much more longs to offer His abundant grace and amazing restoration. So even if it were Bathsheba who had enticed David (a theory some scholars flirt with), how both got into this hubbub is noteworthy only as a teachable moment

---

41 Ibid.

to help us avoid even the very appearance of evil. What is clear is that the two wound up between forbidden sheets and the corporate result was tragic—that itself is powerful!

David could have run away with his tail between his legs, but he didn't. He wrote, "He that covers his sins shall not prosper: but whosoever confesses and forsakes them shall have mercy" (Psalm 28:13). The insidious seed of lust mushroomed into a nightmare for him. It was all about a man in an uncommitted relationship for his own pleasure— that's all! But sin in its infancy is always deceitful and underestimated; we have only to read the story of Adam and Eve in Genesis chapter 2 and onward to see how Satan's entrance into Eve's life was subtle and gradual and the effects so much more devastating than Eve's act of disobedience. Likewise, David's cover-up of Bathsheba's pregnancy and the killing of her husband, Uriah, were so much more egregious than the sin of adultery.

Perhaps you are among the countless numbers who, in an act of solidarity with Bathsheba, would offer to pay her legal bills to have David prosecuted. Perhaps I would be numbered among them. But if I need to take a step back, it's because even though I can't fully relate to David's behavior, my human failings help me identify with David's roller-coaster feelings of guilt and shame. "Create in me a clean heart," he cried as he left it all on the altar before God, "and renew a right spirit within me." David had a mountain of issues, but he also had a wealth of faith—he knew that no matter how vile his actions were God would not turn him away in his brokenness.

> The world's Redeemer accepts people as they are, with all their weaknesses and many faults. But He will wash away their sins and redeem them through His blood … He wants to give restoration and peace to all who come to Him.[42]

---

42 *Happiness Digest*, 14.

So who else can compare to a pardoning God such as Jehovah? When we first met David at his crossroads, the most defining moment in his life, how did he respond? He did not seek to transfer blame; he confessed his sin and was prepared to pay the ultimate price of death for it. How did God respond? He favored David with grace by forgiving him and allowing him to live. God always looks at the heart that man so often cannot understand. When David realized that his heart had been stained by sin, he exclaimed,

> Be gracious to me, O God, according to your loving kindness; according to the greatness of your compassion blot out my transgressions. Wash me thoroughly from my iniquity and cleanse me from my sin. For I know my transgressions, and my sin is ever before me. Against You, You only, I have sinned and done what is evil in your sight. (Psalm 51:1–4)

Hear David again in Psalm 51:7: "Purge me with hyssop and I shall be clean; wash me and I shall be whiter than snow." What a setup for forgiveness, healing, and restoration! Can we understand now why God, in an unprecedented act, named David a man after His own heart? (Acts 13:32).

A Work in Progress

What's in it for you? How can you be delivered from the mess you've made? Even if your failings have been sheet matters in which the notion of purity was placed at the very bottom of your to-do list, you can feel empowered by the authority of God's holy scripture and the indwelling of the Holy Spirit.

> All those the Father gives me will come to me, and whoever comes to me I will never drive away. For I have come down from heaven not to do my will but to do the will of him who sent me. And this is the will of

him who sent me, that I shall lose none of all those he has given me, but raise them up at the last day. (John 6:37–39)

Scripture contains example after example of God showering His grace and mercy on the fallen and granting them second chances.

- » My little children. (1 John 2:12)

- » Draw near to God. (James 4:8)

- » Repent therefore and be converted. (Acts 3:19–21)

- » What man of you having ... (Luke 15:4–6)

- » For the Son of Man is come. (Matthew 18:11–13)

- » Who is a God like unto you. (Micah 7:18–19)

- » Then Peter came to Him and said, "Lord, how often ..." (Matthew 18:21–22)

- » So I will restore to you the years. (Joel 2:25–26)

- » Return. (Jeremiah 3:22)

- » Wash yourselves. (Isaiah 1:16)

- » Restore to me. (Psalm 51:12)

Our faith in God's ability to restore us to Him will increase if we are willing to see ourselves through the lens of characters such as David, the notorious adulterer and murderer (2 Samuel 11), the Samaritan woman with all her baggage and insecurities who did everything she could think of to escape society's ridicule of her revolting life (God "found" her in Luke 10:25–37), and the Prodigal Son, whose father ran to meet him and shower his love on him even though he had left home and had squandered his inheritance (Luke 15:11–32).

God is never far away from those who are willing to know Him.

> He who seeks to quench his thirst at the fountains of this world will drink only to thirst again ... Everywhere

men are unsatisfied. They long for something to supply the need of the soul. Only one can meet that want. The need of the world, "The Desire of all nations," is Christ. The divine grace which He alone can impart, is as living water, purifying, refreshing, and invigorating the soul.[43]

Fully Forgiven, Fully Restored

In humanity's world, pardon is generally contingent upon a quid pro quo—what's in it for me? And the award is often proportionate to the quality and duration of the favor. This is not so with God—He does a thorough job and doesn't triage us but admits us into His finest hospital for His state-of-the-art treatment, the atoning blood of Jesus. He washes us when we come to Him and treats us as if we've never sinned. "If we confess our sins, he is faithful and just and will forgive us our sins and purify us from all unrighteousness" (1 John 1:9).

So when we come to God for forgiveness and restoration, we must come knowing we have exhausted our supply of worldly sources yet nothing could satisfy. We must come believing that the Healer knows about our sheet woes and yearns to do what He does best, save His precious jewels from the Enemy. God's love for us is masterful and authentic, not subject to change in any circumstance. "For God so loved the world that he gave his one and only Son, that whoever believes in him shall not perish but have eternal life" (John 3:16).

Who Is Eligible?

All who seek deliverance should long to become partners with Christ as they determine to surrender their old ways. For some, the place of deliverance is a place of security where shame and hopelessness end and newness begins. It's a place where addictions become "I can do all things through Christ." Think for a moment about the Samaritan

---

43 Desire of Ages, chapter 19.

woman who brought an "empty" life to Jacob's well, expecting to draw common water. After her encounter with Jesus, she scurried to rescue her cohorts from the brothels and to introduce them to a man who knew her darkened heart. Little did this Samaritan outcast know that all the while God was writing her script and her failures were but a footnote to her story.

As you seek to defeat the stronghold of sexual vices and immorality, keep in mind that God is in such hot pursuit after you that no matter how you try to elude Him, He will keep you in plain sight until you surrender and are safe in His arms. What blessed assurance it is to know that God's capacity to clean things up is significantly more powerful than our capacity to mess things up, and that's a blessing!

Chapter Fourteen

E-MAILS FROM GOD ON SEXUAL PURITY

Consider it pure joy, my brothers and sisters, whenever
you face trials of many kinds, because you know that
the testing of your faith produces perseverance.
—JAMES 1:2

What Would God's E-mails on Sexual Purity Look Like?

*I*f you're ever tempted to go up against God on His position on sexual purity, realize that His principles are and will be always the same. God will never relax His Commandments to accommodate fleshly lusts and pacify society's norms; He will never bend to appease anyone.

If we clear the fog from our eyeglasses, we will discover that is it not possible to engage in sexual impurity without committing other related sins such as lying, fornicating, adultery, and covetousness. When we understand that God has no darling sins, we will understand His position is not affected by what's popular and what's not or who's a good, moral person who sometimes pushes the envelope a little when it comes to sexual stuff. "Jesus Christ is the same yesterday and today and forever" (Hebrews 13:8). Every aspect of His character is fixed while others may push the goalposts around to accommodate social norms.

In nearly every discussion I get involved in with young people and more-seasoned Christians, the question is always, "Why has the church become mute on the subject of sexual purity?" Though we ask such a question from church leadership at times like ours, what happens when we get no response? Has the church's voice become weakened or muted because its leaders are unable or unwilling to speak up because their hands have been contaminated by sexual impurity as well? What does this apparent tolerance for immorality mean for Christians, especially young people, as they attempt to salvage what's left of their moral consciences to live upright in the sight of God? What does the church's silence on immorality and sexual purity among believers have on the message of the gospel of Christ?

When the church becomes hushed or worse, numbed, on the subject of sexual purity, it becomes by default part of the problem and believers become ill informed on the standards God expects them to attain. They become emboldened with an aura of "my reality" as they rationalize their decision to engage in sexual inappropriateness in favor of the "Nobody's perfect" line.

God will never cave in to societal pressures or offer anybody any wiggle room. God's clarion call to holiness and right living is as clear today as ever.

> If my people, who are called by my name, will humble themselves and pray and seek my face and turn from their wicked ways, then I will hear from heaven, and I will forgive their sin and will heal their land. (2 Chronicles 7:14)

Imagine waking up, praying, and checking these e-mails.

Inbox—Breaking News! Your Body Is Not Your Own.

Do you not know that your bodies are temples of the Holy Spirit, who is in you, whom you have received from God? You are not your own; you were bought at a price. Therefore honor God with your bodies. (1 Corinthians 6:19–20)

Inbox—Breaking News! You Will Be Tempted.

Brothers and sisters, if someone is caught in a sin, you who live by the Spirit should restore that person gently. But watch yourselves, or you also may be tempted. (Galatians 1:10)

Inbox—Breaking News! Shift Your Focus on God.

Flee the evil desires of youth and pursue righteousness, faith, love and peace, along with those who call on the Lord out of a pure heart. (Timothy 2:22)

Inbox—Breaking News! There Is a Reward For Faithfulness.

Dear friends, now we are children of God, and what we will be has not yet been made known. But we know that when Christ appears, we shall be like him, for we shall see him as he is. All who have this hope in him purify themselves, just as he is pure. (1 John 2:2–3)

Inbox—Breaking News! I'll Stand by You.

I can do all this through him who gives me strength. (Philippians 4:13)

Inbox—Breaking News! I'll Clean You Up.

Hide your face from my sins and blot out all my iniquity. Create in me a pure heart, O God, and renew a steadfast spirit within me. Do not cast me from your presence or take your Holy Spirit from me. (Psalm 51:9–11)

Inbox—Breaking News! I Hereby Charge You …

Let love and faithfulness never leave you; bind them around your neck, write them on the tablet of your heart. Then you will win favor and a good name. (Proverbs 3:1–8)

Inbox—Breaking News! I'll Set You Free.

Therefore, there is now no condemnation for those who are in Christ Jesus, because through Christ Jesus the law of the Spirit who gives life has set you free from the law of sin and death. (Romans 8:1–2)

Inbox—Breaking News! I Hereby Command You …

Flee the evil desires of youth and pursue righteousness, faith, love and peace, along with those who call on the Lord out of a pure heart. (2 Timothy 2:22)

Inbox—Breaking News! Keep Your Heart Pure—I Will Reward You.

Blessed are the pure in heart, for they will see God. (Matthew 5:8)

Reread your e-mails from God and allow the apostle Paul's confident assertion on how to handle the battle between spirit and flesh be the rule. When you do, isn't it possible to attain sexual purity, thus fulfilling the high standards God expects of His children?

So I say, walk by the Spirit, and you will not gratify the desires of the flesh. For the flesh desires what is contrary to the Spirit and the Spirit what is contrary to the flesh. They are in conflict with each other, so that you are not to do whatever you want. (Galatians 5:16–17)

Chapter Fifteen

TAKE OFF YOUR USED-TO-BE SHOES

Brothers and sisters, I do not consider myself yet to have taken hold of it. But one thing I do: Forgetting what is behind and straining toward what is ahead, I press on toward the goal to win the prize for which God has called me heavenward in Christ Jesus.
—PHILIPPIANS 3:13–14

One of the greatest challenges to purity is the fear of being cut from the social roster. It's a fun Saturday night; your clique is out and about if not tucked away in some forbidden place doing forbidden things between forbidden sheets with forbidden persons. You know this either as a fact of your life or because it's not so far removed from your "used to be" life. You're moving forward, but the kinks are not all worked out—desire is strong. In the distance, you hear Paul the vocal apostle say,

> For I know that good itself does not dwell in me, that is, in my sinful nature. For I have the desire to do what is good, but I cannot carry it out. For I do not do the good I want to do, but the evil I do not want to do—this I keep on doing. (Romans 7:18–20)

Yes, even Paul, that awesome follower of Christ, struggled with a sinful nature; that's why at one point in his wrestling with God and himself, he exclaimed in verse 24: "What a wretched man I am! Who will rescue me from this body that is subject to death?" Here is where it pays to have a personal relationship with God. When the flesh is raging and your faith is dim, you will be confident that there is a Father who understands and is willing to deliver you when you're faced with divers temptations. Isn't that good news?

Listen to Paul, who in Romans 7:25 replied to his rhetorical question: "Thanks be to God, who delivers me through Jesus Christ our Lord!" This is the kind of powerful stuff that makes you shout!

The word *fear* raises its ugly head once more because fear is the greatest threat to the freedom we are on our way to be granted. It is perhaps the biggest obstacle to the victory that's looming. Here is what the Enemy tells you: If you fail in your pursuit of purity, you will lose your credibility. If you succeed in your pursuit of purity, it is nigh impossible you will survive socially and a life of loneliness awaits you. So the options are limited but clear—surrender those blemished sheets, be prepared to be a social outcast from your used-to-be clique, surrender all to Jesus, and be set free in His name.

David is on point—there can be no negotiation tactics when you're serious about breaking free. Letting go is war, much like severing ties with a rogue nation. And the same way there are no holds barred in war, breaking free of carnal desires requires putting on the whole armor of God. Lest we become consumed by our own strength, David puts that notion to rest, for in his lamenting before the only true God, he exclaimed, "Cleanse me with hyssop, and I will be clean; wash me, and I will be whiter than snow" (Psalm 51:7).

That's deliverance, my friend—that's where you want to be! When we accept that this world has nothing lasting to offer, we will place less importance on self-gratification and more on things eternal. We understand this, but we would be happy to hold onto the flesh with one hand and pour into a life of purity with the other. But it doesn't work that way. Paul weighed in succinctly.

> Don't you know that friendship with the world means enmity against God? Therefore, anyone who chooses to be a friend of the world becomes an enemy of God.

This is stuff nobody tells you, but when you have finally caught a glimpse of Christ, you reach the place where for the first time you feel your spirit soar, and there are some things you just can't keep to yourself—this is one of them!

But here you are in good company, because neither could the woman at the well remain quiet when she encountered Jesus. Before her encounter, she could not even dream of giving credit to the Master; after her encounter, she not only acknowledged Him but also wanted to share Him and wanted to identify with Him so much so that back in her old neighborhood, she began her first evangelistic series under the theme, "Come see a man who told me everything I ever did!" (John 4:29).

The best-kept secret about the past and what it is possible to become through Christ is this: God knows our names and our spiritual struggles; more than anything, He wants to deliver us from sin, from our independence. He also wants to elevate our status from struggling sinners to sinners saved by His grace.

What If?

Had it not been for her experience at the well, it's likely the Samaritan woman would have drowned in her ocean of despair, victim of a snake that squeezes the sweetness out of its prey leaving no room for the anointing. But ah, morning broke, the fog cleared, and just when the Enemy thought his party was set, the rain of God's mercy began to fall. It was another of those moments when everything in the universe halts when God has a statement to make: "I, the one speaking to you—I am he" (John 4:26).

The Samaritan woman was a willing recipient of God's grace and mercy, for once she realized that light had come, she heeded the call. She knew the water she had been drinking was not thirst-quenching. We can find not one ounce of selfishness in her after her encounter Christ; she had one goal—to share what she had experienced with her circle. Her behavior spoke volumes about her heart; man looks at outward appearances, but God can see and understand the heart.

In another instance of how God allows us to take off our "used to be" shoes, we turn to the woman in John's gospel who was caught in a compromising sexual act. If those self-righteous men who turned in the adulteress woman thought they were scoring big points while trying to trap Jesus, they were wrong. They didn't understand the true character of Christ, who had made it clear in John 6:37, "Whoever comes to me I will never drive away."

Just when the men thought they would revel in one of their finest moments, Jesus turned the tables on them. John 8 recalled that after Jesus had written in the sand, He said, "Let anyone of you who is without sin is the first to throw a stone at her." I can visualize the startled men cowering as they slipped away, "the older ones first until only Jesus was left, with the woman still standing there" (verse 9).

The imagery of Jesus standing up for a "disgraced" adulteress speaks volumes of the extent of His love for even the vilest sinner. That He condemned a sinful act while loving the sinner was amazing! "Then neither do I condemn you," Jesus assured the woman. "Go now and leave your life of sin" (verse 11).

This woman, whose prior life was mired in sexual confusion, gained knowledge of the saving power of Christ. Such is the kind of heart God is searching out to tug at. How many would dare be so bold? For her courage and childlike trust, God pardoned and loved this woman in the midst of those self-righteous Pharisees—and oh how they hated that! Jesus gave this precious woman grace to cover her sin: "Neither do I condemn you, go and sin no more."

How many could so easily defy social order and follow their Lord unabashedly? Remember when you experienced Jesus for the first time and the flurry of questions began? "Why can't I come in for a nightcap?" "Why can't you do the bars anymore?" "Why can't you play my kind of music anymore?" Were you apologetic? Were you unfazed?

Even in your neighborhood, people began to notice your schedule change; you were home more; the jamming in your car changed; you were rocking to a different beat and different lyrics such as "Jesus, all the way" and "What a marvelous thing you've done, Lord!" What's different? You were seeing the world through newer and clearer lenses, and because Christ was tending your nest, His sweet aroma was freshening every room.

A Challenge

Don't believe for one moment that you cannot surrender your guilt-ridden sheets for a life free of undercover deeds. The difficulty is not that what happens between the sheets is so fulfilling, it's your inability to believe you can fully commit to your new way of life. So often we want to add and subtract from the divine equation to make Jesus into a narrative that fits our own story. But we cannot sanitize, rationalize, or marginalize Him. He is who He is, our deliverer who seeks to change us for all time. He is Jehovah God, the Christ who is willing to transform all those who come to Him with even the vilest of issues. That's how God works! If you miss this, you miss out on what your "used to be" shoes symbolize—the fact that God encountered you at the bottom of the pit, extracted you with His love, mercy, and grace, and elevated you to a high plane to do service for Him.

When we anchor our faith in God, whose ability to transform is beyond comprehension, we will realize there is nothing too hard for Him. He who made the heavens and the earth and put the stars in their place can heal, save, and deliver!

Look for confirmation of the power of God in the story of the man who was born blind; understand that his blindness connoted not only the man's physical condition but our spiritual state today. When the Pharisees questioned the legitimacy and authenticity of the blind man's deliverance from a life of sightlessness, he had one simple response: "One thing I do know. I was blind but now I see" (John 9:25).

Sometimes, you have to forget about popular opinion and proceed on divine revelation, never looking to or expecting others to validate your new life. Some things cannot be explained, and to try to dissect the movement of God in the lives of His people is a mistake. Others' opinions are not important. The real test is whether your decision to surrender your "used to be" for a sanctified life can hold its own. Is it dependent on the views of others? Are you prepared to be governed only by the Lord? Your personal testimony is just that, personal—that Christ has found and transformed you, and you can shout from the mountaintop that your life changed!

Nothing can nullify your transformational experience better than joyless people. They serve only one purpose—to tear down and discourage your forward movement. You have to position yourself to "pick up your bed" as soon as the opportunity knocks, and you will be discovered only when you intentionally make yourself visible and available.

The Decision

Are you patiently waiting at your crossroads to be discovered? Are you waiting at the well, the meeting place that was just the beginning of freedom for the woman who was drawing regular water? She didn't know that the best was yet to come and that physical water would be the least of her concerns. Her water pots symbolized her empty vessel; after she discarded them, she received new pots filled to the brim and overflowing. Christ said, "So I say, walk by the Spirit, and you will not gratify the desires of the flesh" (Galatians 5:13). The well, the meeting place, was just the beginning, for when our water pots are filled with the Living Water, there is never a need for earthly refill!

This story blows me away not just because of the woman's sordid escapades; the water pot captures my attention. She didn't "forget" it, she "left" it! When Jesus enters the picture, worldly things we used to cling to pale into insignificance compared to what Christ has to offer. No one has to cajole us; we turn our backs on them as if they were embarrassments. From a spiritual cell to the living well, from run-down motels to mansions up yonder—that's how God can change broken and disturbed hearts.

Can you imagine the powerful testimony of a prostitute returning to her brothel without her water pots to share her testimony of how God through Christ had delivered her from the clutches of low living and placed her on a mountaintop of hope and fulfillment? "Come; see a man who told me everything I ever did, Could this be the Messiah?" (John 4:29). Isn't that exactly what Jesus wants us to say today? That's why He pleads with us to leave our water pots, go back to those "familiar" places of ill repute, and tell His unfiltered story of a personal transformation and possibilities through Him.

Tell Somebody

Whenever God blesses us, He expects us to bless others with our testimony. The Samaritan woman's decision to share the good news of her deliverance from the clutches of sin is a textbook example for evangelism today. Who could possibly be more suitable to bring "them" in than one who has weathered a life of ill repute and scorn? She was so insignificant that to this day she remains nameless, yet Jesus broke with the protocol and customs of the day and met her. Here comes Jesus again, willing to do whatever it takes to make sure we have life and have it more abundantly! Nothing prevents Him from pursuing us. We can't shake Him off; we can't turn Him off with insults; we can't play games with Him thinking He will get tired of us—that's how badly He wants us saved.

The Samaritan woman had filled her void with men, but Jesus didn't call her a prostitute; He was more interested in filling her life with something that would quench her thirst forever—the Living Water! Whether in the brothels or in the church pews, only Christ can fill our pots so that we will never thirst again. "Whoever drinks of the water I give him will never thirst" (John 4:14).

Rahab's Water Pot: A Companion Story

We read of Jesus time and again in the Bible chasing after the write-offs and making them partners in ministry. We see it in the story of Rahab, the innkeeper prostitute in Joshua who protected the two men Joshua had sent from Shittim as spies. We may never find a more fitting example of godly surrender than Rahab's decision to leave her own "water pots" behind and drink of the Living Water. Even though she made her living as a prostitute, there came a time when the defiled sinner and harlot heard about the God of Israel and risked her life to become acquainted with Him. That is undoubtedly why this unlikely Bible character's life is such a poignant metaphor for everyone lost in sin and in search of the Savior.

Can we agree that Rahab had done it all? Though her weaknesses may not be ours, it is not the category or magnitude of sin that defiles—it's sin period! God sacrificed His Son to redeem and sanctify us from whatever our deficit might be. We've lived in a state of "smugness" long enough, debating over which sin is lesser and which is greater; now it's time to refocus on the power of God to take even the vilest sinner and make him or her a part of His family. Now is the time to seek after God's story line with new passion: "You will seek me and find me when you seek me with all your heart" (Jeremiah 29:13).

Had Rahab lived in the twenty-first century, her sexual escapades might have been posted all over Facebook. She might have been the butt of late-night TV jokes, and the church folks in her neighborhood might have spent their Sunday afternoons "juicing" her. But look at her now! She is at a place where her critics would love to be—part of Christ's own family. Christ didn't come to call the righteous but the sinners to repentance. So much of Rahab's life is shrouded in mystery, but we know she had a beginning, we understand all too clearly her sordid in between, and under normal circumstances we might have been able to write the script on Rahab's life—a lady of the night who met a tragic ending perhaps?

Watch God!

When God enters the picture, the flow shifts, and the impossible becomes the miraculous. Rahab moved from rebel to royalty, exactly what God wants you to know is possible in your life. Rahab presented herself again, but this time as an official part of the bloodline of Christ— sins blotted out, past forgiven, clean and made whole, saved for time and for eternity. This obscure, infamous innkeeper took off her "used to be" shoes and was ushered into the bloodline of Christ. Is there anything too hard for God?

You may not reach your new goal of sexual purity in a week or even in a month. You must not give up, however. Think about how the insignificant snail crawls along so slowly but in due time reaches its destination. This is your personal journey—your personal turn-around mission, and in the worst-case condition, you may slip back into your "was" shoes, but keep thinking about one day wearing golden slippers. How does God take broken people and turn them into absolute miracles? Who can tell? But one thing is certain, He does!

No one is justified in throwing stones at others who may be living in sin because everyone is only a stone's throw away from his or her "used to be" life. Everyone has a dog in the purity fight! We are all broken people on a journey to be like Jesus. Therefore, let those who due to the generous grace of God have attained deliverance from their cesspools jump at any opportunity to render aid to others who are discouraged. When we pour ourselves into the lives of others, we are investing in our own spiritual enrichment and growth.

Chapter Sixteen

THE HEART OF A VIRTUOUS WOMAN

A virtuous woman: who can find one?
Not smug in her singleness but content –
Not handicapped by timidity but confident in tenacity –
Not fearful but assured and courageous –
Who can find one?
Her worth is far more valued than earthly treasures –
Her life is crowned with favor –
She rises early in the morning before dawn
And bends her knees before the throne of God …
A virtuous woman—singing, praying, working, waiting for the move
   of God –
Not consumed with worldly bells and whistles, and such
But modest and even-tempered—not envious, nor boastful.
She is prudent in her demeanor and credible in her words –
Her family trusts in her and call her blessed.
Who can find one?
A virtuous woman—model of purity and honor,
At noon and at evening time—from morn to night
Her ways find delight in the things of God –
God's favor paves her path!
A virtuous woman: who can find one?

Chapter Seventeen

FINAL THOUGHTS

In the long run, we shape our lives, and we shape ourselves.
The process never ends until we die. And the choices we
make are ultimately our own responsibility.
—ELEANOR ROOSEVELT

There is a charm about the forbidden that
makes it unspeakably desirable.
—MARK TWAIN

It's a wrap! No one no matter how attractive or statuesque is worth the pain you will experience if you break your covenant with God and refuse to abide by His sheet rules. Society has sold us a shipload of knockoff ideas: "If you don't squeeze the mango before you pick it, you risk buying a dud." "If you really want the mango, you have to let your feelings known by sampling it."

Two elderly men fond of relating fables and mixing metaphors were on a porch musing about the mangoes on a tree several feet away. In a manner characteristic of older gentlemen, he pointed to some pristine mangoes. "Do you know why they're up there and the others are down low?" he asked his companion. Before the friend could reply, the questioner said, "Never pick the ones hanging low—they've been squeezed by too many others."

Isaiah tells us, "But they that wait upon the LORD shall renew their strength; they shall mount up with wings as *eagles*, they shall run and not be weary, and they shall walk and not faint" (Isaiah 40:31). What a powerful symbol of the eagle! You can see it as it flies, hovering far beyond all the other birds. Similarly, God wants the best for His children—let there be no doubt about that. The word *wait* tells us the posture we should take while anticipating His provisions, and the word *mount* could be seen as the power in God's might to persevere to the top. God, who wants the best for His children, grieves when they just hang around the perimeter of blessing. If God wants gold for you, why settle for bronze?

"It is God's will that you should be sanctified: that you should avoid sexual immorality; that each of you should learn to control your own body in a way that is holy and honorable, not in passionate lust like the pagans, who do not know God; and that in this matter no one should wrong or take advantage of a brother or sister. The Lord will punish all those who commit such sins, as we told you and warned you before. For God did not call us to be impure, but to live a holy life."

Before the Sheets: Thirty-Two Things You Must Not Miss

» What? Rehabilitate him? You will make yourself a nonstop nag and eventually destroy your spiritual and physical health. Even after all that, there will be no change. So much for teaching old dogs new tricks.

» Whatever you do, don't shack up! Keep an eye on him. Don't let him sneak his clothes in one shirt at a time. No matter how cold and lonely it gets, don't allow him to sleep over. If he claims he's not feeling well, drive him to the emergency room—not a bad place to lie over.

» Poor communication skills. Do you turn red when he speaks in public? He doesn't necessarily need an Ivy League education, but he must be able to communicate clearly. Can he convey his feelings about important matters? Does he clog up? Mental health professionals agree that apart from money issues, communication is a big reason for breakups.

» Poor sense of humor—easily offended.

» Never trust a guy who can't look you in the eye when he speaks to you. What's he hiding?

» Avoid defensive guys who make you walk on eggshells. If you think a guy with a superiority complex is difficult, try one with an inferiority complex.

» Watch the family. Get to know them. Don't take your lover's word for anything; he will do and say anything to get you. Find out stuff for yourself from ex-wives and ex-girlfriends, sisters and brothers, friends and neighbors. Don't leave it to chance—learn some private-eye skills.

» Watch out for the kind who is easily persuaded by others and wants to be everything to everybody. Can't say no. He's likely not to be able to say no to other women or his family. I call it the "assisted living" phenomenon—always has to get kudos from others, otherwise he does not trust himself. A kind of yo-yo. No right-thinking woman wants to be with not to mention marry a wimp!

» Pay close attention to his value system. If you love the Lord and he couldn't care less, say good-bye. Imagine you want to spend your Wednesday evening at prayer meeting but he's happier at the strip club licking his chops. What's his take on fidelity? On finances? Is it what's mine is mine and what's yours is ours? Does he consult his siblings on personal matters?

» Is he easily provoked? Does he have an anger problem?

» How does he feel about your career? Your talents? Does he support you, or does he feel threatened?

» Is he overly attentive to you? Wink-wink! Does he show signs of desperation, e.g., "I will die if I don't get you …?"

» Does he like kids? Does he relate to them as a father type or as a friend? There's a difference.

» What's his worldview? Can he withstand a decent debate about politics and religion without getting bent out of shape?

» Is he a man or a woman or neither? Don't be fooled if he's been married with a couple of kids; that doesn't mean he's a man. Check out his buddies. There is such a word as "dual."

» Oh gosh—the friend! Watch them! "Birds of a feather flock together."

» Don't be too sweet! Check out his past relationships. Interview as many people as possible. If he's from out of town, consider hiring someone to do an intimate background search for you. For example, chances are good that if he cheated on others, he'll do the same on you. If he had a pattern of domestic violence, it will not stop.

» Is he a cut-and-run person, or does he have an ability to resolve issues? Issues will arise in a relationship, guaranteed.

» Consider a man with the Holy Ghost power. It works pretty well between the sheets.

» Don't trust the roving eye. It suggests that he's attracted to beauty and could well mean he has a zipper problem. True, you want him to see other women as attractive or otherwise, but there is never a positive reason to eyeball them. It's rude, disrespectful, disgusting, and could spell lots of trouble ahead. It also suggests instability.

» Don't be fooled into thinking that in-laws aren't important. Check them out. Watch how they interact with other in-laws. If they will allow you to bond with other sisters- and brothers-in-law, jump at the opportunity. That's a gold mine because they know the scoop.

» A man stuck in the past cannot be trusted. If he claims his old sweethearts are good friends, that's trouble! If they're biddies, that's double trouble. If he's not capable of thinking outside the box, realize you have a dunce on your hands. Let him go!

» Is he a cheapskate? Is he overly extravagant? Either way, you have a problem.

» Is he truthful? One lie may not seem like a big deal, but a liar is a thief/cheat, and a thief/cheat is a murderer.

» Is he obsessed with his hobby? Unless he enjoys making you a part of it, you will probably be a lonely married woman.

» Check out his friends. They speak volumes.

» Do you desire a "churched" guy? Be careful not to spend all your time scrutinizing the doctrine—look at the individual. He could well be a whitened sepulcher inside a worthy church.

» Don't be overcome by good looks. Look first for good character. Good looks will get old, but the inner man lives on. The veneer wears off like designer cologne; it lasts for a while, then what's underneath smells unless it's clean.

» Is he a brawler? Lacking pedigree? Does he

» Some men are professional cheaters. Don't think for one moment that because you are so fine they won't cheat on you. Even if you turn into an angel, they will claim that because you were so angelic, they needed a break. Many men are attracted to "bad" women—they get a rush from living on the edge.

» Never date a married man. If he tells you his marriage is not doing well, introduce him to a shrink. Never assume that role.

If he cheats on his wife with you, he will cheat on you with someone else—guaranteed! That's a character flaw.

Know what you want in a relationship. Not every guy who has a six-figure salary is a good get; there are qualities more important than that. How much is he willing to compromise? Some folks are prepared to accept a whole lot more than others; as an example, some people will accept an extramarital affair because they're having one as well.

"The steps of a good man are ordered by the LORD: and he delights in his way (Psalm 37:23).

REFERENCES

Chapter One—Setting Boundaries

Proverbs 30:15

Deuteronomy 28:13

The Great Controversy @sacred-texts.com

Is American Culture in Decline? Greenhaven Press 2005, 87.

blog.beliefnet.com/news/2011/09/pastor-tells-flock-to-stop-tolerating-adultery-delete-facebook-accounts-shun porn.php#ixzz2ePZLVQ8v

www.drlindahelps.comDating Advice: 10 Dating Tips for Christian Singles

High Moral Standards, August 23, 2010 by Terrie Lynn Bittner, LDS

Blog: bettyconfidential.com/ar/ld/a/What-Do-Men-Really-Think-About-Sex-on-the-First-Date.html#ouZTuvtikhEUzrbR.99;

Ibid.

Ibid.

Romans 8:5

Eugene H. Peterson, The Message (Colorado Springs) Nav. Press, 1993, 1994, 1995, 375 [up]

Ephesians 6:10–18.

Chapter Two—Self-Denial: A Panacea For Purity

James 1:14

Ephesians 5:31

1 Corinthians 7:2

1 Thessalonians 4:3–5

David Peterson, Possessed by God; A New Testament theology of sanctification and holiness, Intervarsity Press, 1995, 82–84.

Genesis 1:26–27

Galatians 6:7

Jeremiah 29:11

Jackie Kendall, *Raising A Lady In Waiting*, 31; D. Priscilla Brown, *Touched by a Galilean*, 54

www.urbandictionary.com/define.php?term=commitment www.summit.org/resources/truth.../the-importance-of-worldview-training;

Daniel 3:17

Jeremiah 29:11

www.christianpost.com/news/what-humpty-dumpty-can-teach-us-about-sexual-purity-79593/#mkOAi8UILZcm0G07.99; Genesis 2:24

Proverbs 22:6

Psychology Today, August 13, 2012, Carolyn C. Ross, M.D., M.P.H. in Real Healing

Proverbs 13:24

Sunday, April 14th, 2013 by WTM.org Community

Psalm 23:3

St. Josemaría Escrivá

Hebrews 13:4; 1 John 1:9

Romans 3:23

2 Corinthians 5:17

Chapter Three—The Nest Does Matter

Kirkland H. Pratt, Counseling Psychologist … Workshop Notes, November 7, 2012

www.piercedhands.com/5-rules-fathers-daughters/ wearethatfamily.com/.../raising-daughters-in-a-world-that-devalues-them...March 20, 2013

Ibid.

Barbara Kasey Smith. Created on: March 04, 2008 and updated October 30, 2012

Philippians 3:13–14

Psalm 27:14

Genesis 17.16–19

Genesis 22:15–18

2 Corinthians 12:9

Luke 14:33

Steps to Christ, Review & Herald publication, p. 43, Youth Edition

www.whiteestate.org/books/sc/sc7.html

Isaiah 43:25.

Chapter Four—Shacking Up Is a Fraud

Genesis 3:2–4

Ibid 4–5

Robert Deffinbaugh,"Let Me See Thy Glory" 1997 Biblical Studies Press, LLC and the authors.

David Popenoe and Barbara Defoe in Divorce Culture and coauthors of the report in the National Marriage Project "Should We Live Together? What Young Adults Need to Know About Cohabitation Before Marriage Crosswalk Family Newsletter (undated)

Review & Herald Publishing Association: "Happiness Digest" p 14

Pratt, K. Horatio, Counseling Psychologist, 2013

Cohabitation in the United States, From Wikipedia, the free encyclopedia;

Genesis 1:1

1 Corinthians 10:13

Chapter Five—Finding Mr. Right: Stuff Nobody Told Me!

Psalm 37:4

Jeremiah 31:3

Blog: God's Assurance/My Utmost for His Highest utmost.org/god's-assurance/Jun 5, 2013

Philippians 4:7

Chapter Six—Guarding the Avenues of the Heart

Proverbs 4:23; Ephesians 5:3; James 1:14–16; 1 Peter 5:8

Mark 14:38 Jeremiah 29:11

Chapter Seven—When Your Desires and God's Will Clash

Romans 1:24 www.gilead.net/egw/books/misc/Steps_to_Christ/5_Consecration;

Eugene H. Peterson, The Message (Colorado Springs) Nav Press, 1993, 1994, 1995, 375 [up]; 2 Corinthians 12:7

White, Steps to Christ, Youth Edition, and p. 40, Review & Herald Publishing Association

Romans 8:7

www.amazingfacts.org/media-library/book/e/.../remember-lots-wife.aspx

www.ewtn.com/library/mother/ma2wills.htm

Eugene H. Peterson, The Message (Colorado Springs) Nav Press, 1993, 1994, 1995, 375 [up].

2 Corinthians12:7

Psalm 34:18

John 4:34

Luke 17:32

Steps to Christ, 58–59, www.whiteestate.org/books/sc/sc7.htm

Romans 12:2

Psalm 37:5–7

Psalm 37:5–7

Isaiah 43:2

Psalm 4:3

Psalm 25:9

Psalm 81:10

Psalm 23:3

Psalm 27:14

Isaiah 30:18

Isaiah 54:17

Psalm 40:3

Chapter Eight—Sheet Secrets: WWJD?

1 Peter 5:8

James 1:17

2 Corinthians 6:14

2 Corinthians 6:17

Revelation 3:17

Exodus 20:3

Matthew 24:35

Hebrews 13:4

Statement of Concern on sexual behavior, the Annual Council of The General Conference of SDA session in Washington, DC, October 12, 1987.

2 Chronicles 7:14

Proverbs 4:23

Chapter Nine—Voices from the Biological Clock

Psalm 37:23

Psalm 37:3–5

Genesis 30:1–2

Jeremiah 29:11

Romans 8:28

Genesis 29:25

2 Corinthians 10:12

Luke 1:30

Genesis 29:35

Philippians 4:11

Genesis 29:17

Genesis 3:5

Julie Hiramine, Guardians of Purity, 164, Chrisma House.

Psalm 27:14

Genesis 17:18,19

SDA Bible Commentary, November 2011

Deuteronomy 7:9

Numbers 23:19

Psalm 27:14

Chapter Ten—Enjoy Your Final Descent

Philippians 4:19

2 Peter 3:9

2 Peter 1:6.

Chapter Eleven—Blemished Sheets and God's Grace

2 Corinthians 12:9

Isaiah 1:18

Galatians 5:17

Galatians 2:20

Genesis 3:19–20

John 4:29

Chapter Twelve—Forgiven

John 10:10

Matthew 18:3

2 Corinthians 5:17

John 8:36

John 8:36

Jeremiah 31:34

Isaiah 43:25

Psalm 32; Matthew 7:1–5

1 Timothy 1:15

Romans 5:10

Psalm 103:2–3

Psalm 103:10–14

2 Corinthians 5:17

Hebrews 9:14

2 Peter 1:9

Colossians 3:13

Hebrews 12:15

Hebrews 4:16

General Conference of SDA Adult Sabbath School Bible Study Guide, 35

Romans 15:13

Philippians 4:8

Chapter Thirteen—Restitution and Restoration

Isaiah 1:18–20

John 3:16

Jeremiah 17:9

Psalm 51:1–14

Psalm 51:1–14

Happiness Digest, p. 10, Discovering the secret of endless joy

Steps to Christ, p 42

Psalm 28:13

Happiness Digest, p. 1

Psalm 51:1–4

Psalm 51:7

1 John 2:12; James 4:8

Acts 3: 19–21

Luke 15:4–6

Micah 7:18–19

Matthew 18:11–13

Joel 2:25–26

Jeremiah 3:22

Isaiah 1:16

Psalm 51:12

2 Samuel 11

Desire of Ages, Chapter 19

Chapter Fourteen—E-mails from God on Sexual Purity

James 1:2

Hebrews 13:8

2 Chronicles 7:14

1 Corinthians 6:19–20

Galatians 1:10

Timothy 2:22

1 John 2:2–3

Philippians 4:13

Psalm 51:9–11

Proverbs 3:1–8

Romans 8:1–2

2 Timothy 2:22

Matthew 5:8

Galatians 5:16–17

Chapter Fifteen—Take Off Your Used-To-Be Shoes

Philippians 3:13–14

Romans 7:18–20

John 4:29

Psalm 51:7

John 4:26

John 9:25

Galatians 5:13

John 4:29

Jeremiah 29:13

Chapter Sixteen—The Heart of a Virtuous Woman

Chapter Seventeen—Final Thoughts

CASE STUDIES

Case Study 1: Should Believers Date or Marry Unbelievers?

Religion News Service (USA Today) and other "credible" news sources report that Christians divorce as much as everyone else in America. Should the news reports be believed?

The Challenge

Think about divorce in the church today. You may not have done a scientific survey, but even anecdotally, divorce in church congregations and even among church pastors is far too common. How does the apparent escalating divorce rate among Christians fit into the biblical vision that Christians should not marry non-Christians?

Consider

> When the Lord your God brings you into the land you are entering to possess and drives out before you many nations—the Hittites, Girgashites, Amorites, Canaanites, Perizzites, Hivites and Jebusites, seven nations larger and stronger than you—and when the Lord your God has delivered them over to you and you have defeated them, then you must destroy them totally. Make no treaty with them, and show them no mercy. Do not intermarry with them. Do not give your daughters

to their sons or take their daughters for your sons, for they will turn your children away from following me to serve other gods, and the Lord's anger will burn against you and will quickly destroy you. (Deuteronomy 7:1–4)

A friend of mine (gun shy as a result of an ill-advised marriage to a nonbeliever of another culture) reluctantly shared some personal moments of her harrowing ordeal. In hindsight, she confessed she advertised a balloon of covert deceptions—she called them "outs" that were clearly designed to justify dating and marrying outside her faith. "Do not be yoked together with unbelievers. For what do righteousness and wickedness have in common? Or what fellowship can light have with darkness?" (2 Corinthians 6:14).

In conducting interviews for this book, I discovered that 100 percent of the 200 couples or individuals interviewed ultimately broke up because of spiritual incompatibility regardless of other possible contributing factors. I shared my findings with two couples both in "other faith" relationships who have been dating for a relatively short time; of course, they were head over heels about each other.

Looking for Clarification

What does it mean to be unequally yoked? Do we mean two people sharing the same faith are automatically perfectly matched for marriage? If yes, how do we explain the failed marriages of folks who shared the same faith? Is there a more complicated question here that needs to be addressed? Is it possible for a couple to share the same faith but not the same values in other key aspects of life?

We have so much intelligence at our fingertips, so let's assume the statute of limitation on stupidity has expired because we can't wrestle with our hips out of joint. Exactly what does it mean to be unequally yoked?

A lifelong pastor friend once chided me with regard to what he perceived as my poor judgment in choosing a lifelong mate: "You spent too much time examining his church and too little time investigating him." I took that to mean that not everyone who's a member of a religious body and is faithfully engaged in churchly activities is necessarily a genuine Christian. Even if he is, is he truly prepared for marriage just because he's of age?

The corresponding assumption is that some who are not truth seekers attend church for nefarious reasons. There is also a "buyer beware" caveat that because an individual is in the church he will not necessarily make a fit spouse. What then? It is prudent to be diligent in dating choices.

Conclusion

Jesus acknowledged there would be counterfeit Christians roaming among His flock: "Woe to you, teachers of the law and Pharisees, you hypocrites! You are like whitewashed tombs, which look beautiful on the outside but on the inside is full of the bones of the dead and everything unclean" (Matthew 23:27). "I am sending you out like sheep among wolves. Therefore be as shrewd as snakes and as innocent as doves" (Matthew 10:16).

Construct your own scenario and discuss with your own small group.

Notable Quotes

Case Study 2: Sex Outside Marriage— Prudish or Sinful?

The Challenge

"Almost all Americans have premarital sex" says a published report that analyzes federal data over time and suggests programs focusing on sexual abstinence until marriage may be unrealistic.[44]

---

44   Public Health Reports, USA TODAY—12/19/2006.

The study, which used statistics from the 1982, 1988, 1995, and 2002 National Survey of Family Growth, questioned about 40,000 individuals ages fifteen to forty-four about their sexual behavior and traced the trends in premarital sex to the 1950s.

The report found that of those interviewed in 2002, 95 percent reported they had had premarital sex; 93 percent said they had done so by age thirty. Among women born in the 1940s, nearly nine in ten did.

How do you reconcile such statistics with biblical teaching on sexual purity? Is there a missing component outside the prevailing assumption that sexual relations outside of marriage are okay?

How do you inform society's carefree thinking on sex out of wedlock? Do the casual attitudes toward sex today dilute the importance of marriage?

Some popular claims: We're not hurting anybody. Everybody is doing it. Sex has incredible health benefits in that it relieves stress, calms nerves, boosts the immune system, burns calories, stimulates the heart, increases self-worth and self-confidence, and reduces the threat of prostate cancer. If God didn't want us to "do it," He would not have made "it."

The Result

When placed in a moral and biblical context and when placed in the context of the effects of "free" or "unbridled" sex on today's society and its impact on societal ills such as divorce, child abuse, and domestic violence, a biblical response to sex outside marriage or at least a thorough examination of the reason for its popularity must be pursued.

Case Study 3: Should Your Biological Clock Determine Your Commitment to Purity?

The Challenge

Is God specific about sexual relations in and outside marriage? Would He cut some slack for ticking biological clocks? The Bible settles this question: "Marriage should be honored by all, and the marriage bed kept pure, for God will judge the adulterer and all the sexually immoral" (Hebrews 13:4).

We have ingested a lot of junk over the years we need to regurgitate and discard. Let's begin to unload with this question and perhaps use it as a foundation: "Is there a biblical basis for the notion that everyone must procreate? Does not God, all-knowing and all-powerful, know whether it is in His divine plan for every person to have children? Is God specific enough about sexual relations within the confines of marriage, and how can we settle the issue once and for all?

Conclusion

Wrestle with these:

Sex was intended solely for procreation.

The Bible prohibits sexual relations within marriage purely for pleasure.

It is sinful for two people who are deeply in love to have sex before marriage.

You can still go to heaven if you have sex before marriage.

Scripture Resources

"You are the salt of the earth. But if the salt loses its saltiness, how can it be made salty again? It is no longer good for anything, except to be thrown out and trampled underfoot" (Matthew 5:13).

"Don't let anyone look down on you because you are young, but set an example for the believers in speech, in conduct, in love, in faith and in purity" (1 Timothy 4:12).

"Do nothing out of selfish ambition or vain conceit. Rather, in humility value others above yourselves, not looking to your own interests but each of you to the interests of the others" (Philippians 2:3).

"If you fully obey the Lord your God and carefully follow all his commands I give you today, the Lord your God will set you high above all the nations on earth. All these blessings will come on you and accompany you if you obey the Lord your God" (Deuteronomy 28:1–3).

"Do you not know that he who unites himself with a prostitute is one with her in body? For it is said, "The two will become one flesh. But whoever is united with the Lord is one with him in spirit. Flee from sexual immorality. All other sins a person commits are outside the body, but whoever sins sexually, sins against their own body" (1 Corinthians 6:18).

"Those who are in the realm of the flesh cannot please God … For if you live according to the flesh, you will die; but if by the Spirit you put to death the misdeeds of the body, you will live" (Romans 8:8, 13).

Case Study 4: Setting Boundaries— Outdated or Enduring?

The Challenge

Let's begin with the story of Isaac and Jacob and two women and their maids in Genesis 29:31 and Genesis 30:24. Read the story and judge for yourself; you will find that TV reality shows and dysfunctional households are nothing new. Jacob was a busy man who was ferried from sheet to sheet. We know hormones were plentiful. It's held that Jacob's attraction to Rachael was purely physical and that Leah was a victim of an unfaithful husband. After reading this story, the notion of setting boundaries in our lives will become clear.

Wrestle with These

If boundaries are unimportant, why are the consequences of "free for all" so great?

Would you be interested in knowing what Jacob's relationship with God was during this period of his life? Might knowing this impact how close you stay to Him at all times?

Was God silent during this debacle in Genesis 29:31 and 30:24? This response will require sober deliberation.

Conclusion

What should our attitude be in the context of this scenario? Jackie is your husband's ex and lives in the same town as your family. Should you become close friends with Jackie? Should your husband remain friends with Jackie? Should your husband spend time alone with Jackie? What does the Bible advise about the above "avoidance" scenario? Read Proverbs 14:16 and 1 Thessalonians 5:19–22 to start.

Case Study 5: Feel Left Out? God Has a Special Love for Single Women

The Challenge

Be willing to face these truisms:

Satan is on steroids and will disrupt the single woman's sexual equilibrium.

You should never lose the warmth of the Holy Spirit just because you are not hooked up with someone of the opposite gender.

The sweet savor of Christ is present in your life, or is it?

There is no in-between—either you are continually withdrawing from your Christlikeness or you are getting your energy from worldliness.

Myra, Miriam, is a powerful servant of God who has influenced countless lives through her ministry. But will bitterness cause her to self-destruct spiritually?

Liddy, Lydia, has been very successful in business, but spiritually, she feels lost. How will she respond when she hears the truth of God?

Winnie, the widow of Zarephath, is a desperate single mother who cannot feed her child. But when God sends her help in an unlikely way, is she willing to trust him enough to take it?

Vera, the widow with the two mites, has fallen on hard times and is living in poverty. When God calls her to take a leap of faith by giving up all she has, will she obey?

Molly, Naomi, is bitter after the tragic deaths of her husband and sons. Will she find hope and help in God?

Annie, Anna, a tireless servant of the Lord, has done His work her whole life. How will the Lord reward her for her devotion?

Marie and Marty, Mary and Martha, are sisters with opposite personalities. One is a go-getter and tireless worker while the other prefers study and conversation. Which personality does God desire more?

Conclusion

For Discussion:

"Do not conform any longer to the pattern of this world, but be transformed by the renewing of your mind. Then you will be able to test and approve what God's will is—his good, pleasing and perfect will" (Romans 12:2).

"She speaks with wisdom, and faithful instruction is on her tongue" (Proverbs 31:26).

Are the temptations of sexual sins more prevalent in single women than in married women?

How does the single Christian woman process her desires?

Christians must understand that because Jesus gave His life for them, sacrifice is enough to keep Him. What about a close, personal relationship with God? Is it important so that constant discourse with Him is possible? Can God stay the temptations of sexual desires?

Is it God's will for everyone to marry?

What does the Bible say about a Christian staying single at any age? Look at Corinthians 7:7–8: "I wish that all men were as I am. But each man has his own gift from God; one has this gift, another has that. Now to the unmarried and the widows I say: It is good for them to stay unmarried, as I am."

Will God give you a definitive answer if you ask Him to reveal His will for your life in terms of remaining single?

Notable Quotes

Case Study 6: Does Walking Away from Getting Hitched Trump Getting Ditched?

The Challenge

You are a Christian, you say; you have faith, you say; you've prayed, you say; you know that the relationship you're in is suffocating—you've even been making wedding plans but you're convinced it's not what God wants for you. Do you go ahead with your plans and hope for the best?

You've dealt with the red flags, but now there are flags of numerous colors flying before your face. However, many social and emotional pressures are keeping you from making that final decision. Do you go back to the drawing board and make a list of concerns and see if you can rationalize them, or do you swallow your embarrassment, suck in your gut, and cut your losses?

Before you make a move, ask yourself, *Why do I want this relationship to continue? Why do I want this relationship to end? Does this relationship have the elements of sound Christian principles in it?*

Choosing the right mate is hard work. Who is suitable? Of course there's no magic formula, but remember that boy in high school you snubbed? He's no longer gangly. Look him up—he's still unhitched, only now he's an accomplished educator who still loves the Lord. Perhaps he'll talk to you!

Young women around the world are thanking Joelle Caputa, author of *Trash the Dress* and *Why Women in Their 20s Get Hitched When They Should've Ditched*. Her books are empowering; her stories are compelling. But why young women in their early and late twenties are marrying every Tom, Dick, and Harry demands probing.

For Discussion

What pushes women in their twenties into ill-advised marriages?

How much is the pressure to marry by age twenty influenced by media and society? By dysfunctional nesting?

Would dating and marriage have far different results if couples adhered to biblical guidelines on intimacy and marriage?

Look again at both early marriages and late marriages. Is one more to be recommended? What do the statistics confirm?

What do you want out of an intimate relationship? What does God want for you out of your intimate relationship?

Think about the parable in Matthew about the house built on rock and the house built on sand. How does this parable relate to the ingredients that must be present in a relationship to ensure it's foundationally strong?

Conclusion

> Therefore everyone who hears these words of mine and puts them into practice is like a wise man who built his house on the rock. The rain came down, the streams rose, and the winds blew and beat against that house;

yet it did not fall, because it had its foundation on the rock. But everyone who hears these words of mine and does not put them into practice is like a foolish man who built his house on sand. The rain came down, the streams rose, and the winds blew and beat against that house, and it fell with a great crash. (Matthew 7:24–27)

Notable Quotes

Case Study 7: Forgiveness: Overstated or Essential?

The Challenge

Snoop for a minute into the bedroom of the Samaritan woman: married five times, currently shacking up, heaven knows what else. To her, the idea of sexual purity was an oxymoron. Nevertheless, Jesus engaged her at the well, and the result of that encounter in John 4 was life altering for her. Jesus looked at her collective mess, forgave her, and in a total role-reversal added urban ministry to her resume.

Take a gamble on a community harlot of Canaan! Who would have imagined that this woman, Rahab, the antithesis of purity, could become a set-apart woman of unequaled virtue having received the honor of kinship in the line of Jesus Christ? And why would a righteous God bestow the honor of sainthood on her?

Paul in 2 Corinthians 12:9 has an explanation—that God's mercy and power is most effectively demonstrated through human frailty. "By faith the prostitute Rahab, because she welcomed the spies, was not killed with those who were disobedient" (Hebrews 11:31).

Conclusion

Jacob and Esau were not identical in personality by a long shot. Esau was rugged and loved outdoor activities such as attending to sheep and hunting. Jacob, in contrast, was a mama's boy interested in the home.

Once, when Jacob was cooking, Esau came in from the open country famished. He said, "Quick! Let me have some! I'm famished!"

Jacob replied, "First sell me your birthright."

"Look, I'm about to die," Esau said. "What good is the birthright to me?"

Jacob said, "Swear to me first."

So Esau swore an oath to Jacob, selling his birthright to him.

Jacob gave Esau bread and lentil stew.

Esau traded his birthright for a bowl of beans.

Jacob's and Esau's lives became entangled in deception. So the time came when the father Isaac realized that he knew he was near death; he requested that his hunter son Esau kill a deer to prepare a good meal before dividing the estate. When Rebecca, the twins' mother, heard the request, she too joined the parade of deception—she helped Jacob pull off a grand scheme to sucker Isaac into bestowing on Jacob the larger portion of the inheritance.

Jacob eventually had to escape to save his life. He found his mother's relatives in another country; they sheltered him and took care of him. He remained with his mother's family for many years before he returned to his own family. Upon his return, Jacob learned that his brother Esau was looking for him. Jacob (the deceiver) was terrified. He devised a plan so that his brother could only destroy half of Jacob's wealth if he was caught. But when they eventually met up, Esau surprisingly ran to Jacob, hugged and kissed him, and demonstrated forgiveness and mercy. But not only did Esau forgive Jacob, his response to his brother was so over-the-top, that there was not even a hint of bitterness between them.

The Samaritan woman, Rahab, and the famous twins, Jacob and Esau—an unlikely foursome on the face of it, but all became powerful examples of the power of forgiveness—each forgiven by a forgiving God.

"For if you forgive other people when they sin against you, your heavenly Father will also forgive you" (Matthew 6:14).

"Get rid of all bitterness, rage and anger, brawling and slander, along with every form of malice. Be kind and compassionate to one another, forgiving each other, just as in Christ God forgave you" (Ephesians 4:31–32).

"My sacrifice, O God, is a broken spirit; a broken and contrite heart you, God, will not despise" (Psalm 51:17).

"Come now, let us settle the matter," says the Lord. "Though your sins are like scarlet, they shall be as white as snow; though they are red as crimson, they shall be like wool" (Isaiah 1:18).

"All this is from God, who reconciled us to himself through Christ and gave us the ministry of reconciliation: that God was reconciling the world to himself in Christ, not counting people's sins against them. And he has committed to us the message of reconciliation" (2 Corinthians 5:18–19).

Notable Quotes

"A forgiveness ought to be like a canceled note, torn in two and burned up, so that it can never be shown against the man." —Henry Ward Beecher

"Man has two great spiritual needs. One is for forgiveness. The other is for goodness." —Billy Graham

Case Study 8: He's Rich—Amen! Are You a Gold Digger?

The Challenge

Have you always dreamed you'd marry a rich man who would give you a lavish life with all the material stuff you could ever use? Do you find yourself consumed with the thought of being rich? Would you choose wealth over looks, or wealth over honor? Does nothing matter as long as there is an abundance of money?

"Money won't make you happy … but everybody wants to find out for themselves." —Zig Ziglar

"Money will say more in one moment than the most eloquent lover can in years." —Henry Fielding

Material Girls

Hot on the teetering heels of the *Sex and the City* movie comes *Priceless*, a film about a woman who seduces a man for his wealth. And real women are increasingly encouraged to do the same via specialized dating websites, a host of "how to" guides, and T-shirts proclaiming the virtues of such a life. Since when was being a gold digger something to aspire to, Sarah Churchwell asks.

Conclusion

"When I surveyed all that my hands had done and what I had toiled to achieve, everything was meaningless, a chasing after the wind; nothing was gained under the sun" (Ecclesiastes 2).

"For the love of money is a root of all kinds of evil. Some people, eager for money, have wandered from the faith and pierced themselves with many griefs" (1 Timothy 6:10).

Notable Quotes

Case Study 9

"The Spirit of the Lord is on me, because he has anointed me to proclaim good news to the poor. He has sent me to proclaim freedom for the prisoner and recovery of sight for the blind, to set the oppressed free, to proclaim the year of the Lord's favor"(John 13:35).

Even if you believe that pornography is harmless, you need to pay close attention to Sarah's story. She was twenty when she fell in love and married her high school sweetheart, Jeremy ...

ELABORATE IN YOUR OWN WORDS AND BE READY FOR GROUP PRESENTATION: Many think pornography has no ill effects, but research has proven that pornography can shape attitudes and encourage behavior that harms ...

Notable Quotes

Case Study 10—Sexual Impurity or Stuffy Saints?

The Challenge

It's hard to tell people that God will forgive them despite the nature or severity of their sin. I soaked in this almost-radical idea when I encountered an unmarried couple in my pew a year ago. Accompanying the couple was their young child. The reason for thinking twice about this couple was not that they were unmarried but that their crude imagery stood out—nose, ears, and eyebrow piercings (at least ten), tattoos on every inch of exposed flesh, and bright orange and purple hair. This is how the couple presented. I said a grudging hello to them not because I was comfortable doing so but because their toddler was precocious and engaging, continuously playing with the beads on my purse.

It's greeting time: "I'm so glad I'm a part of the family of God ... I've been washed in the fountain, cleansed by His blood ... joint heirs with Jesus as we travel this sod, for I'm glad I'm a part of the family of God." That was the welcome song that filled the air as members showered hugs and kisses on each others' cheeks as they mingled.

But something stood out like a sore thumb—the odd couple were ignored during the circulating; actually, they were on their feet trying to mouth the song. No one noticed, including me.

The singing was tapering off along with the cheerfulness, and just as I was moving back to my seat, the young lady who later identified herself as Emma looked me in the eye and with a look of expected reciprocity, buried her head in my neck. "I love you," she whispered. "I love you too," I replied with measured interest.

Thus began my friendship with a lovely couple and their toddler, now a preschooler, who deeply love the Lord. To this day, I cherish my friendship with that unsuspecting family and will do anything to revisit that worship service just to undo the profiling of a family who were also God's property.

I still ask myself how Jesus would have treated that couple when He first encountered them. I had made the faulty assumption many Christians make every day about people who are different in lifestyle or appearance. Is it safe to say that this scenario is commonplace in churches throughout society? Is it a picture that should ignite a firestorm of discussion and examination? (The couple, as it turned out, were "new babes in Christ" and were transitioning from their worldly personae to the tamer profile the body of Christ offered.)

What do we know about purity? Could an obviously impure person surrender to Christ and become pure, as if he or she had never sinned? Let's look at a definition of sin before we see whether Emma and her significant other were just as righteous as that joyful congregation if not more so.

What is sin? It's disobedience to God's Commandments either by doing what is forbidden or failing to do what is required. Sin undermines and disrupts our relationship with God and separates us from His love.

What part does forgiveness when we disobey God? We want to look to what Jesus says about how He treats those who violate His Commandments. Luke 15:3–7 tells us,

Then Jesus told them this parable: "Suppose one of you has a hundred sheep and loses one of them. Doesn't he leave the ninety-nine in the open country and go after the lost sheep until he finds it? And when he finds it, he joyfully puts it on his shoulders and goes home. Then he calls his friends and neighbors together and says, 'Rejoice with me; I have found my lost sheep.' I tell you that in the same way there will be more rejoicing in heaven over one sinner who repents than over ninety-nine righteous persons who do not need to repent."

The Solution

The good news is that no matter how serious the sin, God is always seeking us out and is willing to forgive and forget our sins and give us a fresh start. As long as we live, it's never too late to ask for forgiveness and make a new start.

For Discussion

"Then I acknowledged my sin to you and did not cover up my iniquity. I said, I will confess my transgressions to the LORD. And you forgave the guilt of my sin" (Psalm 32:5).

"And forgive us our debts, as we also have forgiven our debtors. And lead us not into temptation, but deliver us from the evil one. For if you forgive other people when they sin against you, your heavenly Father will also forgive you. But if you do not forgive others their sins, your Father will not forgive your sins" (Matthew 6:12–15).

"I am writing to you, dear children, because your sins have been forgiven on account of his name" (1 John 2:12)

"When you were dead in your sins and in the uncircumcision of your flesh, God made you alive with Christ. He forgave us all our sins" (Colossians 2:13).

Notable Quotes

Too often we try to bring God in on the tail end of things and have the chutzpah to expect him to bless our out-of-His-will decision. Well, God isn't a bookmark we stick in the middle of a chapter; He is the alpha and the omega, the beginning of all things, a jealous God who gets a front-row seat or will be a no-show.

From early adolescence, a girl has to be perfectly clear about what she wants. Nobody told me that stuff, but if there isn't clarity in what she wants, chances are excellent she will settle for what someone else wants her to be, which will always be less than her potential. If you don't stand for something, you will fall for anything, including a gigolo, a swindler, or a hoodlum. Don't accept what others define you as—know yourself and accentuate what you like about yourself.

Girls display emotional dishonesty when they pretend they're fine on the outside but inwardly feel like fifty cents. Parents must train their girls to discover their inner selves.

Don't leave the scene of the accident—when the Officer arrives, He will clear up the mess.

Speed bumps are installed for a reason.

Questions You've Been Asking

Highlights from fascinating moments with Doreen Priscilla Brown on her journey from early years to *Wrinkled Sheets and God's Grace:*

Some of you who have read my other books *Move Mountain Move* and *Touched by a Galilean* know my story of humble beginnings and a challenging childhood, how at age eight, I was afflicted with a lethal disease that left me comatose for several weeks. Though at one point the doctors pronounced me clinically dead, the Great Physician had other plans—I miraculously survived, though partially paralyzed and unable to take more than a couple steps at a time. But the miracle didn't end there; the journey to recovery took many months of intensive therapy (the longest nine months of my life), but a sweet soul of an aunt, thankfully a nurse by profession, lovingly nursed me.

Unless you have undergone the Lazarus experience—thought to be clinically dead only to be brought back to life again—it would be difficult to comprehend how the experience informs one's psyche even at the tender age of eight. On November 7, 1957, one day before my birthday, I opened my eyes with a smile on my face (they tell me at the break of dawn) and asked for a slice of cantaloupe.

The miracle still didn't end there. I returned to elementary school and went on to high school without a single absence, and I graduated with a near-perfect grade point average after the medical team had said I would be "unable to learn."

But the miracle did not stop there; the same medical team blew it again. "She will never be able to have children," they told my aunt reluctantly. But look how God works: many years later, three perfect pregnancies and three brilliant children!

Today, I'm standing on the promises of God, blood-bought and sold out for Christ, the honored recipient of His grace, mercy, and forgiveness!

When folks hear my story, they often say, "You're so lucky!" But that's what they think; I know better. For me, luck is something that happens by chance. I say that the fact I write to you is nothing less than a miracle! And what do you do when the Master Miracle Worker favors you with a second chance? You appreciate it, become thankful for it, cherish it, and use the experience as testimony to encourage others to pursue God's Word, mindful of Philippians 1:6: "Being confident of this, that he who began a good work in you will carry it on to completion until the day of Christ Jesus."

I'm in a secure place—I'm confident; I know Christ in a personal way, fully aware that God works in mysterious ways. For His divine reasons, He has permitted a young girl to experience the worst of life so she may inspire others to move from fetal positions to experiencing the best life yet. I love the Lord very much, so I have purposed in my heart to dedicate my whole life to Him, leaving everything I have on the battlefield.

God is particular about His instructions to His children; and just as speed bumps are meant to us slow down, when God asks us to follow a specific path meticulously laid out for us, He expects us to comply precisely as He commands, without modification to His admonitions to suit our carnal desires. Hence, it was out of my profound supernatural experiences that *Wrinkled Sheets and God's Grace* emerged. Obedience. Virtue. Purity. Restoration. Perseverance. Patience. Long-suffering. Self-control. Ultimately, a forgiving God who loves us even at our worst and who desires that we pursue the prize of purity as we wait on Him for His perfect match—this is the stuff I wished somebody had told me!

If you've missed the chance to get your sheet stuff right the first time, there might not be a need to sound the alarm—my God is a forgiving God, and even when others ignore their bloopers and criticize your "sheet" decisions, the God of second chances will roll up beside you and affirm you.

Keep this truth close to your breast: Being pure does not necessarily mean that you cannot reclaim your honor after a mess-up. Know this: you absolutely can experience a do-over from the point of your slipup; for the matter of purity is not just of a sexual nature but also a spiritual attitude and a heart for a compassionate God who "has called you out of darkness into his wonderful light" (1 Peter 2:9).

My burning desire, therefore, is for this book to be read by all, young and old, mothers and fathers who must guide their children from the cradle up to the sheets and beyond. They must not shun their sacred responsibility, and even when topics seem awkward, they must not excuse themselves. Communicate! Ask God to help you. My prayer is that *Wrinkled Sheets and God's Grace* will encourage you to remove the veil of denial from your minds and stop at nothing to see that your precious pearls are equipped to face a vicious, sexually obsessed society. Above all, arm your children with a godly foundation and your blessings.

Parents: "Children are a heritage from the LORD, offspring a reward from him. Like arrows in the hands of a warrior are children born in one's youth. Blessed (Psalm 127:3–5). "Start children off on the way they should go, and even when they are old they will not turn from it" (Proverbs 22:6).

Children: "Honor your father and mother so that you may live long in the land the LORD your God is giving you" (Exodus 20:12). "Come, my children, listen to me; I will teach you the fear of the LORD.

Whoever of you loves life and desires to see many good days, keep your tongue" (Psalm 34:11–16).

These things you must do and all your efforts will be well pleasing to God.